King Lear
Annotation-Friendly Edition

William Shakespeare

This book is also available in large-print, extra large print and dyslexia-friendly editions

firestonebooks.com

King Lear
Annotation-Friendly Edition
William Shakespeare

2019 Edition

Published by Firestone Books

ISBN-13: 9781796719666

firestonebooks.com

You can also find out more by following Firestone Books on Facebook and Twitter

Contents

A Quick Guide to Successful Annotating

- Write down any thoughts you have as you go along
- Highlight key points, either with a highlighter or by underlining
- Note any literary techniques in the margins. (The *Glossary of Literary Terms* at the back of the book should help)
- Define any words you don't understand – it will help you later
- Look for patterns, such as repeating words and phrases
- Pick out key points that show a character's development
- Summarise your thoughts on the blank pages at the end of each act
- Once you've finished reading the play, go back and add to your notes. In particular look at foreshadowing, echoing and motifs

William Shakespeare – A Brief Biography

William Shakespeare was born in Stratford-upon-Avon, the son of John Shakespeare, a successful glove-maker, and Mary Arden, the daughter of a prosperous farmer. His date of birth is unknown but he was baptised, most likely within a few days of his birth, on 26th April 1564.

It is likely that Shakespeare attended the King's New School in Stratford-upon-Avon where he would have received a classical education. He did not attend university, and at the age of eighteen he married Anne Hathaway who was eight years his senior. Six months later, in May 1583, Anne gave birth to a daughter, Susanna. In 1585 Anne also gave birth to twins, Hamnet and Judith.

Between 1585 and 1592 almost nothing is known of Shakespeare's life, the so called "lost years". Many apocryphal tales about this period have been reported including that he fled his hometown for London to escape prosecution for deer poaching, that he started his theatrical career minding the horses of wealthy theatregoers, and that he may have been briefly employed as a schoolmaster in Lancashire.

By 1592 Shakespeare was an established playwright, with several of his plays having been staged in London. It is also the year that fellow playwright, Robert Greene, published his infamous *Groats-Worth of Wit* in which he attacked Shakespeare for trying to match the writing of university educated writers such as Christopher Marlowe and Thomas Nashe.

In 1596, Shakespeare's only son, Hamnet, died, and while in later years Shakespeare's daughters would marry and have four children between them, none of Shakespeare's grandchildren would have children of their own, and so in 1670 with the death of his granddaughter, Elizabeth, his direct line was ended.

Shakespeare's plays were only performed by the Lord Chamberlain's Men, a company of actors, in which Shakespeare had a share. In 1599 some members of the Lord Chamberlain's Men built their own theatre on the south bank of the river Thames and named it the Globe. As a shareholder in this theatre, holding up to 3000 spectators, Shakespeare became a wealthy man.

Prior to 1599 Shakespeare had only written two tragedies: *Titus Andronicus* and *Romeo and Juliet*, with his focus being more on comedies, history plays and poems. After 1599 he almost stopped writing history plays and instead switched to writing tragedies, writing many of his finest plays including: *Hamlet, Othello, King Lear* and *Macbeth.*

In 1603 the new king, James I, awarded the Lord Chamberlain's Men a royal patent and the company changed its name to the King's Men.

As well as writing plays, Shakespeare also wrote two long poems and a collection of sonnets. The sonnets describe two love affairs, but who these lovers were – or even if they were real or imagined – remains a mystery.

As Shakespeare was also an actor, it meant that rather than working on his plays in isolation he would have worked closely with other actors. Many of the plots for the plays came from history books, or earlier Italian tales, so it is difficult, if not impossible, to work out what contributions were Shakespeare's. Even when he'd finished a particular play, it was still likely to be re-worked by actors and others – something that is done to this day, and keeps his work as fresh and interesting as its ever been.

Though Shakespeare worked as a writer and actor

in London for most of his adult life, his did spend much of his time in Stratford-upon-Avon where, in 1597, he bought New Place as his family home. It's known that Shakespeare was still working as an actor in London in 1608, and that he also retired to Stratford 'some years before his death'.

Shakespeare died on the 23rd of April 1616, around the time of his 52nd birthday. It was said by John Ward, the vicar of Stratford, writing in the mid-1600s that 'Shakespeare, Drayton and Ben Johnson had a merry meeting and, it seems, drank too hard, for Shakespeare died of a fever there contracted.'

Shakespeare was buried at the Holy Trinity Church, the place of his baptism over half a century earlier. The epitaph on his gravestone has a curse against disturbing his resting place:

Good friend, for Jesus' sake forbear,
To dig the dust enclosed here.
Blessed be the man that spares these stones,
And cursed be he that moves my bones.

Fellow dramatist, Ben Johnson, famously and presciently referred to Shakespeare as being 'not of an age, but for all time.' Since his death Shakespeare's reputation has grown, leading him to now be widely regarded as the greatest writer in the English language and the world's greatest dramatist.

Introduction

If you have not read *King Lear*, you may be best off returning to this introduction after you have read the play, or watching it online.

King Lear is an uncomfortable tale of brutality and madness and death, where goodness is seldom rewarded. It is so dark that in later centuries it was often given a happy ending for audiences who were unsettled by the bleak, depressing tone of Shakespeare's original.

Perhaps it should be mentioned that is some sense it is not *Shakespeare's* original. He would have already been familiar with the semi-mythical king, and this can be seen when comparing his play to earlier writings like *King Leir* written by an unknown dramatist, and Raphael Holinshed's *Chronicles of England, Scotland, and Ireland,* published between 1577 and 1587. Raphael Holinshed's *Chronicles* was a source for a number of Shakespeare's plays, including *King Lear, Macbeth* and *Cymbeline*, as well as plays by other great dramatists including Christopher Marlowe.

It isn't known when Shakespeare wrote King Lear but the earliest *known* performance was held in December 1606, and it is likely that there were performances prior to this date. This first known performance was likely to have taken place, like so many of Shakespeare's plays, at the Globe Theatre. The earliest known version of this tale was written by Geoffrey of Monmouth in his *Historia Regum Britanniae* in the twelfth century – which Holinshed used for his *Chronicles*. In Geoffrey of Monmouth's early version, in stark contrast to Shakespeare's play, the ending is a happy one and Cordelia restores her father to the throne. In fact, of all the versions of this play, Shakespeare alone condemns Cordelia to death.

King Lear is among Shakespeare's more complicated plays with two intertwining plots – the main story relating to Lear and his three daughters, and a sub-plot concerning Gloucester and his two sons, the gullible Edgar and the formidable and scheming Edmund.

In *King Lear*, Shakespeare depicts the gradual descent into madness of the title character. The ageing Lear decides to divide his realm among his three daughters, and that this division will be based on their love for him. His two eldest daughters, Goneril and Regan, flatter him with insincere compliments, while Lear's beloved daughter, Cordelia, does not indulge him with overpraise and simply says that she loves him as a daughter should. Enraged at her apparent coldness, Lear disowns her, and instead divides his kingdom between the conniving Goneril and Regan. Cordelia crosses the English Channel and marries the king of France, and after Goneril and Regan plot to kill their father Cordelia returns to England with an army of French troops to do battle with them. Cordelia is defeated and killed, and Lear cradles his daughter's body, his descent into madness complete. Finally, exhausted and heart-broken, he falls dead upon the body of his beloved daughter.

Due to the subject matter of the play, *King Lear* was politically controversial during the period of King George III's mental illness – so much so that it was not performed in London's two professional theatres between 1811 and 1820, the year George III died.

Cordelia, despite only appearing in the first and final acts, seems ever present during the play, and this virtuous daughter of King Lear is one of Shakespeare's finest and well-known heroines.

King Lear is one of William Shakespeare's most complex and fascinating characters; a heady mixture of pride, despair, self-pity and wilfulness; remorse, compassion and empathy; love and madness. It is this mixture, and the evolution, or perhaps regression, of his ever-changing character that make him both a very difficult character for actors to play, and at the same time King Lear is a role coveted by many of the world's most accomplished actors.

Lear's absent-mindedness might seem comic, and his madness tragic. In King Lear as in life, the border between sanity and insanity is blurred.

King Lear was written at a time when forty was considered old, and this connection between senility and old age (Lear was "four score and upward") is perhaps more relevant today than when the play was first written. Now that people are living longer than ever, dementia and other mental illnesses are more prevalent, with dementia having now overtaken heart disease as the UK's biggest killer.

King Lear is a dark and disturbing play, and perhaps no moment is more tragic than in that final scene when we see King Lear cradling his Cordelia's dead body in his arms. Nobel Prize winning playwright George Bernard Shaw wrote: "No man will ever write a better tragedy than Lear"

King Lear still remains relevant today with themes not just of mental illness, but of other topics like misogyny and sibling rivalry. This classic play, and one of Shakespeare's best known, has been adapted for stage, radio and screen numerous times and is as popular today as it was when first published over four hundred years ago.

David Lear
Editor – Firestone Books

KING LEAR

Dramatis Personae

LEAR, King of Britain

KING OF FRANCE

DUKE OF BURGUNDY

DUKE OF CORNWALL

DUKE OF ALBANY

EARL OF KENT

EARL OF GLOUCESTER

EDGAR, Son to Gloucester

EDMUND, Bastard Son to Gloucester

CURAN, a Courtier

Oswald, Steward to Goneril

Old Man, Tenant to Gloucester

Doctor

Fool

An Officer, employed by Edmund

A Gentleman, Attendant on Cordelia

A Herald

Servants to Cornwall

GONERIL, daughter to Lear

REGAN, daughter to Lear

CORDELIA, daughter to Lear

Knights of Lear's Train, Officers, Messengers, Soldiers and Attendants

purpose.

Give me the map there. Know that we have divided

In three our kingdom: and 'tis our fast intent

To shake all cares and business from our age;

Conferring them on younger strengths, while we

Unburden'd crawl toward death. Our son of Cornwall,

And you, our no less loving son of Albany,

We have this hour a constant will to publish

Our daughters' several dowers, that future strife

May be prevented now. The princes, France and Burgundy,

Great rivals in our youngest daughter's love,

Long in our court have made their amorous sojourn,

And here are to be answer'd. Tell me, my daughters,–

Since now we will divest us both of rule,

Interest of territory, cares of state,–

Which of you shall we say doth love us most?

That we our largest bounty may extend

Where nature doth with merit challenge. Goneril,

Our eldest-born, speak first.

GONERIL: Sir, I love you more than words can wield the matter;

Dearer than eye-sight, space, and liberty;

Beyond what can be valued, rich or rare;

No less than life, with grace, health, beauty, honour;

As much as child e'er loved, or father found;

A love that makes breath poor, and speech unable;

Beyond all manner of so much I love you.

CORDELIA: [Aside] What shall Cordelia do?

Love, and be silent.

LEAR: Of all these bounds, even from this line to this,

With shadowy forests and with champains rich'd,

With plenteous rivers and wide-skirted meads,

We make thee lady: to thine and Albany's issue

Be this perpetual. What says our second daughter,

Our dearest Regan, wife to Cornwall? Speak.

REGAN: Sir, I am made

Of the self-same metal that my sister is,

And prize me at her worth. In my true heart

I find she names my very deed of love;

Only she comes too short: that I profess

Myself an enemy to all other joys,

Which the most precious square of sense

possesses;

And find I am alone felicitate

In your dear highness' love.

CORDELIA: [Aside] Then poor Cordelia!

And yet not so; since, I am sure, my love's

More richer than my tongue.

LEAR: To thee and thine hereditary ever

Remain this ample third of our fair kingdom;

No less in space, validity, and pleasure,

Than that conferr'd on Goneril. Now, our joy,

Although the last, not least; to whose young love

The vines of France and milk of Burgundy

Strive to be interess'd; what can you say to draw

A third more opulent than your sisters? Speak.

CORDELIA: Nothing, my lord.

LEAR: Nothing!

CORDELIA: Nothing.

LEAR: Nothing will come of nothing: speak

again.

CORDELIA: Unhappy that I am, I cannot heave

My heart into my mouth: I love your majesty

According to my bond; nor more nor less.

LEAR: How, how, Cordelia! mend your speech a little,

Lest it may mar your fortunes.

CORDELIA: Good my lord,

You have begot me, bred me, loved me: I

Return those duties back as are right fit,

Obey you, love you, and most honour you.

Why have my sisters husbands, if they say

They love you all? Haply, when I shall wed,

That lord whose hand must take my plight shall carry

Half my love with him, half my care and duty:

Sure, I shall never marry like my sisters,

To love my father all.

LEAR: But goes thy heart with this?

CORDELIA: Ay, good my lord.

LEAR: So young, and so untender?

CORDELIA: So young, my lord, and true.

LEAR: Let it be so; thy truth, then, be thy dower:

For, by the sacred radiance of the sun,

The mysteries of Hecate, and the night;

By all the operation of the orbs

From whom we do exist, and cease to be;

Here I disclaim all my paternal care,

Propinquity and property of blood,

And as a stranger to my heart and me

Hold thee, from this, for ever. The barbarous Scythian,

Or he that makes his generation messes

To gorge his appetite, shall to my bosom

Be as well neighbour'd, pitied, and relieved,

As thou my sometime daughter.

KENT: Good my liege,–

LEAR: Peace, Kent!

Come not between the dragon and his wrath.

I loved her most, and thought to set my rest

On her kind nursery. Hence, and avoid my sight!

So be my grave my peace, as here I give

Her father's heart from her! Call France; who stirs?

Call Burgundy. Cornwall and Albany,

With my two daughters' dowers digest this third:

Let pride, which she calls plainness, marry her.

I do invest you jointly with my power,

Pre-eminence, and all the large effects

That troop with majesty. Ourself, by monthly course,

With reservation of a hundred knights,

By you to be sustain'd, shall our abode

Make with you by due turns. Only we still retain

The name, and all the additions to a king;

The sway, revenue, execution of the rest,

Beloved sons, be yours: which to confirm,

This coronet part betwixt you.

[*Giving the crown*]

KENT: Royal Lear,

Whom I have ever honour'd as my king,

Loved as my father, as my master follow'd,

As my great patron thought on in my prayers,–

LEAR: The bow is bent and drawn, make from

the shaft.

KENT: Let it fall rather, though the fork invade

The region of my heart: be Kent unmannerly,

When Lear is mad. What wilt thou do, old man?

Think'st thou that duty shall have dread to speak,

When power to flattery bows? To plainness

honour's bound,

When majesty stoops to folly. Reverse thy doom;

And, in thy best consideration, cheque

This hideous rashness: answer my life my

judgment,

Thy youngest daughter does not love thee least;

Nor are those empty-hearted whose low sound

Reverbs no hollowness.

LEAR: Kent, on thy life, no more.

KENT: My life I never held but as a pawn

To wage against thy enemies; nor fear to lose it,

Thy safety being the motive.

LEAR: Out of my sight!

KENT: See better, Lear; and let me still remain

The true blank of thine eye.

LEAR: Now, by Apollo,–

KENT: Now, by Apollo, king,

Thou swear'st thy gods in vain.

LEAR: O, vassal! miscreant!

[*Laying his hand on his sword*]

ALBANY and CORNWALL: Dear sir, forbear.

KENT: Do:

Kill thy physician, and the fee bestow

Upon thy foul disease. Revoke thy doom;

Or, whilst I can vent clamour from my throat,

I'll tell thee thou dost evil.

LEAR: Hear me, recreant!

On thine allegiance, hear me!

Since thou hast sought to make us break our

vow,

Which we durst never yet, and with strain'd pride

To come between our sentence and our power,

Which nor our nature nor our place can bear,

Our potency made good, take thy reward.

Five days we do allot thee, for provision

To shield thee from diseases of the world;

And on the sixth to turn thy hated back

Upon our kingdom: if, on the tenth day following,

Thy banish'd trunk be found in our dominions,

The moment is thy death. Away! by Jupiter,

This shall not be revoked.

KENT: Fare thee well, king: sith thus thou wilt appear,

Freedom lives hence, and banishment is here.

[*To CORDELIA*]

The gods to their dear shelter take thee, maid,

That justly think'st, and hast most rightly said!

[*To REGAN and GONERIL*]

And your large speeches may your deeds approve,

That good effects may spring from words of love.

Thus Kent, O princes, bids you all adieu;

He'll shape his old course in a country new.

[*Exit*]

[*Flourish. Re-enter GLOUCESTER, with FRANCE, BURGUNDY, and Attendants*]

GLOUCESTER: Here's France and Burgundy, my noble lord.

LEAR: My lord of Burgundy.

We first address towards you, who with this king

Hath rivall'd for our daughter: what, in the least,

Will you require in present dower with her,

Or cease your quest of love?

BURGUNDY: Most royal majesty,

I crave no more than what your highness offer'd,

Nor will you tender less.

LEAR: Right noble Burgundy,

When she was dear to us, we did hold her so;

But now her price is fall'n. Sir, there she stands:

If aught within that little seeming substance,

Or all of it, with our displeasure pieced,

And nothing more, may fitly like your grace,

She's there, and she is yours.

BURGUNDY: I know no answer.

LEAR: Will you, with those infirmities she owes,

Unfriended, new-adopted to our hate,

Dower'd with our curse, and stranger'd with our

oath,

Take her, or leave her?

BURGUNDY: Pardon me, royal sir;

Election makes not up on such conditions.

LEAR: Then leave her, sir; for, by the power that

made me, I tell you all her wealth.

[*To FRANCE*]

For you, great king,

I would not from your love make such a stray,

To match you where I hate; therefore beseech

you

To avert your liking a more worthier way

Than on a wretch whom nature is ashamed

Almost to acknowledge hers.

FRANCE: This is most strange,

That she, that even but now was your best

object,

The argument of your praise, balm of your age,

Most best, most dearest, should in this trice of

time

Commit a thing so monstrous, to dismantle

So many folds of favour. Sure, her offence

Must be of such unnatural degree,

That monsters it, or your fore-vouch'd affection

Fall'n into taint: which to believe of her,

Must be a faith that reason without miracle

Could never plant in me.

CORDELIA: I yet beseech your majesty,–

If for I want that glib and oily art,

To speak and purpose not; since what I well

intend,

I'll do't before I speak,–that you make known

It is no vicious blot, murder, or foulness,

No unchaste action, or dishonour'd step,

That hath deprived me of your grace and favour;

But even for want of that for which I am richer,

A still-soliciting eye, and such a tongue

As I am glad I have not, though not to have it

Hath lost me in your liking.

LEAR: Better thou

Hadst not been born than not to have pleased

me better.

FRANCE: Is it but this,–a tardiness in nature

Which often leaves the history unspoke

That it intends to do? My lord of Burgundy,

What say you to the lady? Love's not love

When it is mingled with regards that stand

Aloof from the entire point. Will you have her?

She is herself a dowry.

BURGUNDY: Royal Lear,

Give but that portion which yourself proposed,

And here I take Cordelia by the hand,

Duchess of Burgundy.

LEAR: Nothing: I have sworn; I am firm.

BURGUNDY: I am sorry, then, you have so lost
a father

That you must lose a husband.

CORDELIA: Peace be with Burgundy!

Since that respects of fortune are his love,

I shall not be his wife.

FRANCE: Fairest Cordelia, that art most rich,
being poor;

Most choice, forsaken; and most loved,
despised!

Thee and thy virtues here I seize upon:

Be it lawful I take up what's cast away.

Gods, gods! 'tis strange that from their cold'st
neglect

My love should kindle to inflamed respect.

Thy dowerless daughter, king, thrown to my
chance,

Is queen of us, of ours, and our fair France:

Not all the dukes of waterish Burgundy

Can buy this unprized precious maid of me.

Bid them farewell, Cordelia, though unkind:

Thou losest here, a better where to find.

LEAR: Thou hast her, France: let her be thine;

for we

Have no such daughter, nor shall ever see

That face of hers again. Therefore be gone

Without our grace, our love, our benison.

Come, noble Burgundy.

[*Flourish. Exeunt all but FRANCE, GONERIL,*

REGAN, and CORDELIA]

FRANCE: Bid farewell to your sisters.

CORDELIA: The jewels of our father, with

wash'd eyes

Cordelia leaves you: I know you what you are;

And like a sister am most loath to call

Your faults as they are named. Use well our

father:

To your professed bosoms I commit him

But yet, alas, stood I within his grace,

I would prefer him to a better place.

So, farewell to you both.

REGAN: Prescribe not us our duties.

GONERIL: Let your study

Be to content your lord, who hath received you

At fortune's alms. You have obedience scanted,

And well are worth the want that you have

wanted.

CORDELIA: Time shall unfold what plaited

cunning hides:

Who cover faults, at last shame them derides.

Well may you prosper!

FRANCE: Come, my fair Cordelia.

[*Exeunt FRANCE and CORDELIA*]

GONERIL: Sister, it is not a little I have to say of

what most nearly appertains to us both. I think

our father will hence to-night.

REGAN: That's most certain, and with you; next

month with us.

GONERIL: You see how full of changes his age

is; the observation we have made of it hath not

been little: he always loved our sister most; and

with what poor judgment he hath now cast her off

appears too grossly.

REGAN: 'Tis the infirmity of his age: yet he hath

ever but slenderly known himself.

GONERIL: The best and soundest of his time

hath been but rash; then must we look to receive from his age, not alone the imperfections of long-engraffed condition, but therewithal the unruly waywardness that infirm and choleric years bring with them.

REGAN: Such unconstant starts are we like to have from him as this of Kent's banishment.

GONERIL: There is further compliment of leavetaking between France and him. Pray you, let's hit together: if our father carry authority with such dispositions as he bears, this last surrender of his will but offend us.

REGAN: We shall further think on't.

GONERIL: We must do something, and i' the heat.

[Exeunt]

SCENE II. The Earl of Gloucester's castle.

[Enter EDMUND, with a letter]

EDMUND: Thou, nature, art my goddess; to thy law
My services are bound. Wherefore should I
Stand in the plague of custom, and permit

The curiosity of nations to deprive me,

For that I am some twelve or fourteen moon-

shines

Lag of a brother? Why bastard? wherefore base?

When my dimensions are as well compact,

My mind as generous, and my shape as true,

As honest madam's issue? Why brand they us

With base? with baseness? bastardy? base,

base?

Who, in the lusty stealth of nature, take

More composition and fierce quality

Than doth, within a dull, stale, tired bed,

Go to the creating a whole tribe of fops,

Got 'tween asleep and wake? Well, then,

Legitimate Edgar, I must have your land:

Our father's love is to the bastard Edmund

As to the legitimate: fine word,–legitimate!

Well, my legitimate, if this letter speed,

And my invention thrive, Edmund the base

Shall top the legitimate. I grow; I prosper:

Now, gods, stand up for bastards!

[Enter GLOUCESTER]

GLOUCESTER: Kent banish'd thus! and France

in choler parted!

And the king gone to-night! subscribed his
power!

Confined to exhibition! All this done

Upon the gad! Edmund, how now! what news?

EDMUND: So please your lordship, none.

[*Putting up the letter*]

GLOUCESTER: Why so earnestly seek you to
put up that letter?

EDMUND: I know no news, my lord.

GLOUCESTER: What paper were you reading?

EDMUND: Nothing, my lord.

GLOUCESTER: No? What needed, then, that
terrible dispatch of it into your pocket? the quality
of nothing hath not such need to hide itself. Let's
see: come, if it be nothing, I shall not need
spectacles.

EDMUND: I beseech you, sir, pardon me: it is a
letter from my brother, that I have not all o'er-
read; and for so much as I have perused, I find it
not fit for your o'er-looking.

GLOUCESTER: Give me the letter, sir.

EDMUND: I shall offend, either to detain or give
it. The contents, as in part I understand them,
are to blame.

GLOUCESTER: Let's see, let's see.

EDMUND: I hope, for my brother's justification, he wrote this but as an essay or taste of my virtue.

GLOUCESTER: [Reads] *'This policy and reverence of age makes the world bitter to the best of our times; keeps our fortunes from us till our oldness cannot relish them. I begin to find an idle and fond bondage in the oppression of aged tyranny; who sways, not as it hath power, but as it is suffered. Come to me, that of this I may speak more. If our father would sleep till I waked him, you should half his revenue for ever, and live the beloved of your brother, EDGAR.'* Hum–conspiracy!–*'Sleep till I waked him,–you should enjoy half his revenue,'*–My son Edgar! Had he a hand to write this? a heart and brain to breed it in?–When came this to you? Who brought it?

EDMUND: It was not brought me, my lord; there's the cunning of it; I found it thrown in at the casement of my closet.

GLOUCESTER: You know the character to be your brother's?

EDMUND: If the matter were good, my lord, I durst swear it were his; but, in respect of that, I would fain think it were not.

GLOUCESTER: It is his.

EDMUND: It is his hand, my lord; but I hope his heart is not in the contents.

GLOUCESTER: Hath he never heretofore sounded you in this business?

EDMUND: Never, my lord: but I have heard him oft maintain it to be fit, that, sons at perfect age, and fathers declining, the father should be as ward to the son, and the son manage his revenue.

GLOUCESTER: O villain, villain! His very opinion in the letter! Abhorred villain! Unnatural, detested, brutish villain! worse than brutish! Go, sirrah, seek him; I'll apprehend him: abominable villain! Where is he?

EDMUND: I do not well know, my lord. If it shall please you to suspend your indignation against my brother till you can derive from him better testimony of his intent, you shall run a certain course; where, if you violently proceed against him, mistaking his purpose, it would make a great gap in your own honour, and shake in pieces the heart of his obedience. I dare pawn down my life for him, that he hath wrote this to feel my affection to your honour, and to no further pretence of danger.

GLOUCESTER: Think you so?

EDMUND: If your honour judge it meet, I will place you where you shall hear us confer of this, and by an auricular assurance have your satisfaction; and that without any further delay than this very evening.

GLOUCESTER: He cannot be such a monster–

EDMUND: Nor is not, sure.

GLOUCESTER: To his father, that so tenderly and entirely loves him. Heaven and earth! Edmund, seek him out: wind me into him, I pray you: frame the business after your own wisdom. I would unstate myself, to be in a due resolution.

EDMUND: I will seek him, sir, presently: convey the business as I shall find means and acquaint you withal.

GLOUCESTER: These late eclipses in the sun and moon portend no good to us: though the wisdom of nature can reason it thus and thus, yet nature finds itself scourged by the sequent effects: love cools, friendship falls off, brothers divide: in cities, mutinies; in countries, discord; in palaces, treason; and the bond cracked 'twixt son and father. This villain of mine comes under the prediction; there's son against father: the king falls from bias of nature; there's father against child. We have seen the best of our time: machinations, hollowness, treachery, and all ruinous disorders, follow us disquietly to our graves. Find out this villain, Edmund; it shall lose thee nothing; do it carefully. And the noble and true-hearted Kent banished! His offence, honesty! 'Tis strange.

[*Exit*]

EDMUND: This is the excellent foppery of the world, that, when we are sick in fortune,—often the surfeit of our own behaviour,—we make guilty of our disasters the sun, the moon, and the stars: as if we were villains by necessity; fools by heavenly compulsion; knaves, thieves, and treachers, by spherical predominance; drunkards, liars, and adulterers, by an enforced obedience of planetary influence; and all that we are evil in, by a divine thrusting on: an admirable evasion of whoremaster man, to lay his goatish disposition to the charge of a star! My father compounded with my mother under the dragon's tail; and my nativity was under Ursa major; so that it follows, I am rough and lecherous. Tut, I should have been that I am, had the maidenliest star in the firmament twinkled on my bastardizing. Edgar–

[*Enter EDGAR*]

And pat he comes like the catastrophe of the old comedy: my cue is villanous melancholy, with a sigh like Tom o' Bedlam. O, these eclipses do portend these divisions! Fa, sol, la, mi.

EDGAR: How now, brother Edmund! what serious contemplation are you in?

EDMUND: I am thinking, brother, of a prediction I read this other day, what should follow these eclipses.

EDGAR: Do you busy yourself about that?

EDMUND: I promise you, the effects he writes of succeed unhappily; as of unnaturalness between the child and the parent; death, dearth, dissolutions of ancient amities; divisions in state,

menaces and maledictions against king and
nobles; needless diffidences, banishment of
friends, dissipation of cohorts, nuptial breaches,
and I know not what.

EDGAR: How long have you been a sectary
astronomical?

EDMUND: Come, come; when saw you my
father last?

EDGAR: Why, the night gone by.

EDMUND: Spake you with him?

EDGAR: Ay, two hours together.

EDMUND: Parted you in good terms? Found you
no displeasure in him by word or countenance?

EDGAR: None at all.

EDMUND: Bethink yourself wherein you may
have offended him: and at my entreaty forbear
his presence till some little time hath qualified the
heat of his displeasure; which at this instant so
rageth in him, that with the mischief of your
person it would scarcely allay.

EDGAR: Some villain hath done me wrong.

EDMUND: That's my fear. I pray you, have a
continent
forbearance till the spied of his rage goes slower;

and, as I say, retire with me to my lodging, from
whence I will fitly bring you to hear my lord
speak: pray ye, go; there's my key: if you do stir
abroad, go armed.

EDGAR: Armed, brother!

EDMUND: Brother, I advise you to the best; go
armed: I am no honest man if there be any good
meaning towards you: I have told you what I
have seen and heard; but faintly, nothing like the
image and horror of it: pray you, away.

EDGAR: Shall I hear from you anon?

EDMUND: I do serve you in this business.

[*Exit EDGAR*]

A credulous father! and a brother noble,
Whose nature is so far from doing harms,
That he suspects none: on whose foolish
honesty
My practices ride easy! I see the business.
Let me, if not by birth, have lands by wit:
All with me's meet that I can fashion fit.

[*Exit*]

SCENE III. The Duke of Albany's palace.

[*Enter GONERIL, and OSWALD, her steward*]

GONERIL: Did my father strike my gentleman for chiding of his fool?

OSWALD: Yes, madam.

GONERIL: By day and night he wrongs me; every hour
He flashes into one gross crime or other,
That sets us all at odds: I'll not endure it:
His knights grow riotous, and himself upbraids us
On every trifle. When he returns from hunting,
I will not speak with him; say I am sick:
If you come slack of former services,
You shall do well; the fault of it I'll answer.

OSWALD: He's coming, madam; I hear him.

[*Horns within*]

GONERIL: Put on what weary negligence you please,
You and your fellows; I'll have it come to question:
If he dislike it, let him to our sister,
Whose mind and mine, I know, in that are one,
Not to be over-ruled. Idle old man,

That still would manage those authorities

That he hath given away! Now, by my life,

Old fools are babes again; and must be used

With cheques as flatteries,–when they are seen

abused.

Remember what I tell you.

OSWALD: Well, madam.

GONERIL: And let his knights have colder looks

among you;

What grows of it, no matter; advise your fellows

so:

I would breed from hence occasions, and I shall,

That I may speak: I'll write straight to my sister,

To hold my very course. Prepare for dinner.

[*Exeunt*]

SCENE IV. A hall in the same.

[*Enter KENT, disguised*]

KENT: If but as well I other accents borrow,

That can my speech defuse, my good intent

May carry through itself to that full issue

For which I razed my likeness. Now, banish'd

Kent,

If thou canst serve where thou dost stand condemn'd,

So may it come, thy master, whom thou lovest,

Shall find thee full of labours.

[*Horns within. Enter LEAR, Knights, and Attendants*]

LEAR: Let me not stay a jot for dinner; go get it ready.

[*Exit an Attendant*]

How now! what art thou?

KENT: A man, sir.

LEAR: What dost thou profess? what wouldst thou with us?

KENT: I do profess to be no less than I seem; to serve him truly that will put me in trust: to love him that is honest; to converse with him that is wise, and says little; to fear judgment; to fight when I cannot choose; and to eat no fish.

LEAR: What art thou?

KENT: A very honest-hearted fellow, and as poor as the king.

LEAR: If thou be as poor for a subject as he is for a king, thou art poor enough. What wouldst thou?

KENT: Service.

LEAR: Who wouldst thou serve?

KENT: You.

LEAR: Dost thou know me, fellow?

KENT: No, sir; but you have that in your countenance which I would fain call master.

LEAR: What's that?

KENT: Authority.

LEAR: What services canst thou do?

KENT: I can keep honest counsel, ride, run, mar a curious tale in telling it, and deliver a plain message bluntly: that which ordinary men are fit for, I am qualified in; and the best of me is diligence.

LEAR: How old art thou?

KENT: Not so young, sir, to love a woman for singing, nor so old to dote on her for any thing: I have years on my back forty eight.

LEAR: Follow me; thou shalt serve me: if I like thee no worse after dinner, I will not part from thee yet. Dinner, ho, dinner! Where's my knave? my fool? Go you, and call my fool hither.

[*Exit an Attendant*]

[*Enter OSWALD*]

You, you, sirrah, where's my daughter?

OSWALD: So please you,–

[*Exit*]

LEAR: What says the fellow there? Call the clotpoll back.

[*Exit a Knight*]

Where's my fool, ho? I think the world's asleep.

[*Re-enter Knight*]

How now! where's that mongrel?

Knight: He says, my lord, your daughter is not well.

LEAR: Why came not the slave back to me when I called him.

Knight: Sir, he answered me in the roundest manner, he would not.

LEAR: He would not!

Knight: My lord, I know not what the matter is; but, to my judgment, your highness is not entertained with that ceremonious affection as you were wont; there's a great abatement of kindness appears as well in the general dependants as in the duke himself also and your daughter.

LEAR: Ha! sayest thou so?

Knight: I beseech you, pardon me, my lord, if I be mistaken; for my duty cannot be silent when I think your highness wronged.

LEAR: Thou but rememberest me of mine own conception: I have perceived a most faint neglect of late; which I have rather blamed as mine own jealous curiosity than as a very pretence and purpose of unkindness: I will look further into't. But where's my fool? I have not seen him this two days.

Knight: Since my young lady's going into France, sir, the fool hath much pined away.

LEAR: No more of that; I have noted it well. Go you, and tell my daughter I would speak with her.

[*Exit an Attendant*]

Go you, call hither my fool.

[*Exit an Attendant*]

[*Re-enter OSWALD*]

O, you sir, you, come you hither, sir: who am I, sir?

OSWALD: My lady's father.

LEAR: 'My lady's father'! my lord's knave: your whoreson dog! you slave! you cur!

OSWALD: I am none of these, my lord; I

beseech your pardon.

LEAR: Do you bandy looks with me, you rascal?

[*Striking him*]

OSWALD: I'll not be struck, my lord.

KENT: Nor tripped neither, you base football player.

[*Tripping up his heels*]

LEAR: I thank thee, fellow; thou servest me, and I'll love thee.

KENT: Come, sir, arise, away! I'll teach you differences: away, away! if you will measure your lubber's length again, tarry: but away! go to; have you wisdom? so.

[*Pushes OSWALD out*]

LEAR: Now, my friendly knave, I thank thee: there's earnest of thy service.

[*Giving KENT money*]

[*Enter Fool*]

Fool: Let me hire him too: here's my coxcomb.

[*Offering KENT his cap*]

LEAR: How now, my pretty knave! how dost thou?

Fool: Sirrah, you were best take my coxcomb.

KENT: Why, fool?

Fool: Why, for taking one's part that's out of favour: nay, an thou canst not smile as the wind sits, thou'lt catch cold shortly: there, take my coxcomb: why, this fellow has banished two on's daughters, and did the third a blessing against his will; if thou follow him, thou must needs wear my coxcomb. How now, nuncle! Would I had two coxcombs and two daughters!

LEAR: Why, my boy?

Fool: If I gave them all my living, I'ld keep my coxcombs myself. There's mine; beg another of thy daughters.

LEAR: Take heed, sirrah; the whip.

Fool: Truth's a dog must to kennel; he must be whipped out, when Lady the brach may stand by the fire and stink.

LEAR: A pestilent gall to me!

Fool: Sirrah, I'll teach thee a speech.

LEAR: Do.

Fool: Mark it, nuncle:

Have more than thou showest,

Speak less than thou knowest,

Lend less than thou owest,

Ride more than thou goest,

Learn more than thou trowest,

Set less than thou throwest;

Leave thy drink and thy whore,

And keep in-a-door,

And thou shalt have more

Than two tens to a score.

KENT: This is nothing, fool.

Fool: Then 'tis like the breath of an unfee'd lawyer; you gave me nothing for't. Can you make no use of nothing, nuncle?

LEAR: Why, no, boy; nothing can be made out of nothing.

Fool: [To KENT] Prithee, tell him, so much the rent of his land comes to: he will not believe a fool.

LEAR: A bitter fool!

Fool: Dost thou know the difference, my boy, between a bitter fool and a sweet fool?

LEAR: No, lad; teach me.

Fool: That lord that counsell'd thee

To give away thy land,

Come place him here by me,

Do thou for him stand:

The sweet and bitter fool

Will presently appear;

The one in motley here,

The other found out there.

LEAR: Dost thou call me fool, boy?

Fool: All thy other titles thou hast given away;

that thou wast born with.

KENT: This is not altogether fool, my lord.

Fool: No, faith, lords and great men will not let

me; if I had a monopoly out, they would have

part on't: and ladies too, they will not let me have

all fool to myself; they'll be snatching. Give me

an egg, nuncle, and I'll give thee two crowns.

LEAR: What two crowns shall they be?

Fool: Why, after I have cut the egg i' the middle,

and eat up the meat, the two crowns of the egg.

When thou clovest thy crown i' the middle, and

gavest away both parts, thou borest thy ass on

thy back o'er the dirt: thou hadst little wit in thy

bald crown, when thou gavest thy golden one

away. If I speak like myself in this, let him be

whipped that first finds it so.

[*Singing*]

Fools had ne'er less wit in a year;

For wise men are grown foppish,

They know not how their wits to wear,

Their manners are so apish.

LEAR: When were you wont to be so full of
songs, sirrah?

Fool: I have used it, nuncle, ever since thou
madest thy daughters thy mothers: for when thou
gavest them the rod, and put'st down thine own
breeches,

[*Singing*]

Then they for sudden joy did weep,

And I for sorrow sung,

That such a king should play bo-peep,

And go the fools among.

Prithee, nuncle, keep a schoolmaster that can
teach thy fool to lie: I would fain learn to lie.

LEAR: An you lie, sirrah, we'll have you
whipped.

Fool: I marvel what kin thou and thy daughters
are: they'll have me whipped for speaking true,
thou'lt have me whipped for lying; and
sometimes I am whipped for holding my peace. I
had rather be any kind o' thing than a fool: and
yet I would not be thee, nuncle; thou hast pared
thy wit o' both sides, and left nothing i' the

middle: here comes one o' the parings.

[*Enter GONERIL*]

LEAR: How now, daughter! what makes that frontlet on?

Methinks you are too much of late i' the frown.

Fool: Thou wast a pretty fellow when thou hadst no need to care for her frowning; now thou art an O without a figure: I am better than thou art now; I am a fool, thou art nothing.

[*To GONERIL*]

Yes, forsooth, I will hold my tongue; so your face bids me, though you say nothing.

Mum, mum,

He that keeps nor crust nor crum,

Weary of all, shall want some.

[*Pointing to LEAR*]

That's a shealed peascod.

GONERIL: Not only, sir, this your all-licensed fool,

But other of your insolent retinue

Do hourly carp and quarrel; breaking forth

In rank and not-to-be endured riots. Sir,

I had thought, by making this well known unto you,

To have found a safe redress; but now grow
fearful,

By what yourself too late have spoke and done.

That you protect this course, and put it on

By your allowance; which if you should, the fault

Would not 'scape censure, nor the redresses
sleep,

Which, in the tender of a wholesome weal,

Might in their working do you that offence,

Which else were shame, that then necessity

Will call discreet proceeding.

Fool: For, you trow, nuncle,

The hedge-sparrow fed the cuckoo so long,

That it's had it head bit off by it young.

So, out went the candle, and we were left
darkling.

LEAR: Are you our daughter?

GONERIL: Come, sir,

I would you would make use of that good
wisdom,

Whereof I know you are fraught; and put away

These dispositions, that of late transform you

From what you rightly are.

Fool: May not an ass know when the cart

draws the horse? Whoop, Jug! I love thee.

LEAR: Doth any here know me? This is not
Lear:

Doth Lear walk thus? speak thus? Where are his
eyes?

Either his notion weakens, his discernings

Are lethargied—Ha! waking? 'tis not so.

Who is it that can tell me who I am?

Fool: Lear's shadow.

LEAR: I would learn that; for, by the
marks of sovereignty, knowledge, and reason,

I should be false persuaded I had daughters.

Fool: Which they will make an obedient father.

LEAR: Your name, fair gentlewoman?

GONERIL: This admiration, sir, is much o' the
savour

Of other your new pranks. I do beseech you

To understand my purposes aright:

As you are old and reverend, you should be
wise.

Here do you keep a hundred knights and
squires;

Men so disorder'd, so debosh'd and bold,

That this our court, infected with their manners,

Shows like a riotous inn: epicurism and lust

Make it more like a tavern or a brothel

Than a graced palace. The shame itself doth speak

For instant remedy: be then desired

By her, that else will take the thing she begs,

A little to disquantity your train;

And the remainder, that shall still depend,

To be such men as may besort your age,

And know themselves and you.

LEAR: Darkness and devils!

Saddle my horses; call my train together:

Degenerate bastard! I'll not trouble thee.

Yet have I left a daughter.

GONERIL: You strike my people; and your disorder'd rabble

Make servants of their betters.

[*Enter ALBANY*]

LEAR: Woe, that too late repents,–

[*To ALBANY*]

O, sir, are you come?

Is it your will? Speak, sir. Prepare my horses.

Ingratitude, thou marble-hearted fiend,

More hideous when thou show'st thee in a child

Than the sea-monster!

ALBANY: Pray, sir, be patient.

LEAR: [To GONERIL] Detested kite! thou liest.

My train are men of choice and rarest parts,

That all particulars of duty know,

And in the most exact regard support

The worships of their name. O most small fault,

How ugly didst thou in Cordelia show!

That, like an engine, wrench'd my frame of

nature

From the fix'd place; drew from heart all love,

And added to the gall. O Lear, Lear, Lear!

Beat at this gate, that let thy folly in,

[*Striking his head*]

And thy dear judgment out! Go, go, my people.

ALBANY: My lord, I am guiltless, as I am

ignorant

Of what hath moved you.

LEAR: It may be so, my lord.

Hear, nature, hear; dear goddess, hear!

Suspend thy purpose, if thou didst intend

To make this creature fruitful!

Into her womb convey sterility!

Dry up in her the organs of increase;

And from her derogate body never spring

A babe to honour her! If she must teem,

Create her child of spleen; that it may live,

And be a thwart disnatured torment to her!

Let it stamp wrinkles in her brow of youth;

With cadent tears fret channels in her cheeks;

Turn all her mother's pains and benefits

To laughter and contempt; that she may feel

How sharper than a serpent's tooth it is

To have a thankless child! Away, away!

[*Exit*]

ALBANY: Now, gods that we adore, whereof

comes this?

GONERIL: Never afflict yourself to know the

cause;

But let his disposition have that scope

That dotage gives it.

[*Re-enter LEAR*]

LEAR: What, fifty of my followers at a clap!

Within a fortnight!

ALBANY: What's the matter, sir?

LEAR: I'll tell thee:

[*To GONERIL*]

Life and death! I am ashamed

That thou hast power to shake my manhood
thus;
That these hot tears, which break from me
perforce,
Should make thee worth them. Blasts and fogs
upon thee!
The untented woundings of a father's curse
Pierce every sense about thee! Old fond eyes,
Beweep this cause again, I'll pluck ye out,
And cast you, with the waters that you lose,
To temper clay. Yea, it is come to this?
Let is be so: yet have I left a daughter,
Who, I am sure, is kind and comfortable:
When she shall hear this of thee, with her nails
She'll flay thy wolvish visage. Thou shalt find
That I'll resume the shape which thou dost think
I have cast off for ever: thou shalt,
I warrant thee.

[*Exeunt LEAR, KENT, and Attendants*]

GONERIL: Do you mark that, my lord?

ALBANY: I cannot be so partial, Goneril,
To the great love I bear you,–

GONERIL: Pray you, content. What, Oswald, ho!
[*To the Fool*]

You, sir, more knave than fool, after your master.

Fool: Nuncle Lear, nuncle Lear, tarry and take
the fool with thee.

A fox, when one has caught her,

And such a daughter,

Should sure to the slaughter,

If my cap would buy a halter:

So the fool follows after.

[*Exit*]

GONERIL: This man hath had good counsel:–a
hundred knights!

'Tis politic and safe to let him keep

At point a hundred knights: yes, that, on every
dream,

Each buzz, each fancy, each complaint, dislike,

He may enguard his dotage with their powers,

And hold our lives in mercy. Oswald, I say!

ALBANY: Well, you may fear too far.

GONERIL: Safer than trust too far:

Let me still take away the harms I fear,

Not fear still to be taken: I know his heart.

What he hath utter'd I have writ my sister

If she sustain him and his hundred knights

When I have show'd the unfitness,–

[*Re-enter OSWALD*]

How now, Oswald!

What, have you writ that letter to my sister?

OSWALD: Yes, madam.

GONERIL: Take you some company, and away to horse:

Inform her full of my particular fear;

And thereto add such reasons of your own

As may compact it more. Get you gone;

And hasten your return.

[*Exit OSWALD*]

No, no, my lord,

This milky gentleness and course of yours

Though I condemn not, yet, under pardon,

You are much more attask'd for want of wisdom

Than praised for harmful mildness.

ALBANY: How far your eyes may pierce I can not tell:

Striving to better, oft we mar what's well.

GONERIL: Nay, then—

ALBANY: Well, well; the event.

[*Exeunt*]

SCENE V. Court before the same.

[*Enter LEAR, KENT, and Fool*]

LEAR: Go you before to Gloucester with these letters.

Acquaint my daughter no further with any thing you know than comes from her demand out of the letter.

If your diligence be not speedy, I shall be there afore you.

KENT: I will not sleep, my lord, till I have delivered your letter.

[*Exit*]

Fool: If a man's brains were in's heels, were't not in danger of kibes?

LEAR: Ay, boy.

Fool: Then, I prithee, be merry; thy wit shall ne'er go slip-shod.

LEAR: Ha, ha, ha!

Fool: Shalt see thy other daughter will use thee kindly; for though she's as like this as a crab's like an apple, yet I can tell what I can tell.

LEAR: Why, what canst thou tell, my boy?

Fool: She will taste as like this as a crab does to

a crab. Thou canst tell why one's nose stands i' the middle on's face?

LEAR: No.

Fool: Why, to keep one's eyes of either side's nose; that what a man cannot smell out, he may spy into.

LEAR: I did her wrong–

Fool: Canst tell how an oyster makes his shell?

LEAR: No.

Fool: Nor I neither; but I can tell why a snail has a house.

LEAR: Why?

Fool: Why, to put his head in; not to give it away to his daughters, and leave his horns without a case.

LEAR: I will forget my nature. So kind a father! Be my horses ready?

Fool: Thy asses are gone about 'em. The reason why the seven stars are no more than seven is a pretty reason.

LEAR: Because they are not eight?

Fool: Yes, indeed: thou wouldst make a good fool.

LEAR: To take 't again perforce! Monster

ingratitude!

Fool: If thou wert my fool, nuncle, I'ld have thee beaten for being old before thy time.

LEAR: How's that?

Fool: Thou shouldst not have been old till thou hadst been wise.

LEAR: O, let me not be mad, not mad, sweet heaven

Keep me in temper: I would not be mad!

[*Enter Gentleman*]

How now! are the horses ready?

Gentleman: Ready, my lord.

LEAR: Come, boy.

Fool: She that's a maid now, and laughs at my departure,

Shall not be a maid long, unless things be cut shorter.

[*Exeunt*]

My Notes

ACT II

SCENE I. A Court within the Castle of the Earl of GLOUCESTER.

[*Enter EDMUND and CURAN, meeting*]

EDMUND: Save thee, Curan.

CURAN: And you, sir. I have been with your father, and given him notice that the Duke of Cornwall and Regan his duchess will be here with him this night.

EDMUND: How comes that?

CURAN: Nay, I know not. You have heard of the news abroad; I mean the whispered ones, for they are yet but ear-kissing arguments?

EDMUND: Not I pray you, what are they?

CURAN: Have you heard of no likely wars toward, 'twixt the Dukes of Cornwall and Albany?

EDMUND: Not a word.

CURAN: You may do, then, in time. Fare you well, sir.

[*Exit*]

EDMUND: The duke be here to-night? The better! best!

This weaves itself perforce into my business.

My father hath set guard to take my brother;

And I have one thing, of a queasy question,

Which I must act: briefness and fortune, work!

Brother, a word; descend: brother, I say!

[*Enter EDGAR*]

My father watches: O sir, fly this place;

Intelligence is given where you are hid;

You have now the good advantage of the night:

Have you not spoken 'gainst the Duke of

Cornwall?

He's coming hither: now, i' the night, i' the haste,

And Regan with him: have you nothing said

Upon his party 'gainst the Duke of Albany?

Advise yourself.

EDGAR: I am sure on't, not a word.

EDMUND: I hear my father coming: pardon me:

In cunning I must draw my sword upon you

Draw; seem to defend yourself; now quit you

well.

Yield: come before my father. Light, ho, here!

Fly, brother. Torches, torches! So, farewell.

[*Exit EDGAR*]

Some blood drawn on me would beget opinion.

[*Wounds his arm*]

Of my more fierce endeavour: I have seen drunkards

Do more than this in sport. Father, father!

Stop, stop! No help?

[*Enter GLOUCESTER, and Servants with torches*]

GLOUCESTER: Now, Edmund, where's the villain?

EDMUND: Here stood he in the dark, his sharp sword out,

Mumbling of wicked charms, conjuring the moon

To stand auspicious mistress,–

GLOUCESTER: But where is he?

EDMUND: Look, sir, I bleed.

GLOUCESTER: Where is the villain, Edmund?

EDMUND: Fled this way, sir. When by no means he could–

GLOUCESTER: Pursue him, ho! Go after.

[*Exeunt some Servants*]

By no means what?

EDMUND: Persuade me to the murder of your lordship;

But that I told him, the revenging gods

'Gainst parricides did all their thunders bend;

Spoke, with how manifold and strong a bond

The child was bound to the father; sir, in fine,

Seeing how loathly opposite I stood

To his unnatural purpose, in fell motion,

With his prepared sword, he charges home

My unprovided body, lanced mine arm:

But when he saw my best alarum'd spirits,

Bold in the quarrel's right, roused to the
encounter,

Or whether gasted by the noise I made,

Full suddenly he fled.

GLOUCESTER: Let him fly far:

Not in this land shall he remain uncaught;

And found—dispatch. The noble duke my master,

My worthy arch and patron, comes to-night:

By his authority I will proclaim it,

That he which finds him shall deserve our
thanks,

Bringing the murderous coward to the stake;

He that conceals him, death.

EDMUND: When I dissuaded him from his intent,

And found him pight to do it, with curst speech

I threaten'd to discover him: he replied,

'Thou unpossessing bastard! dost thou think,

If I would stand against thee, would the reposal

Of any trust, virtue, or worth in thee

Make thy words faith'd? No: what I should deny,—

As this I would: ay, though thou didst produce

My very character,—I'ld turn it all

To thy suggestion, plot, and damned practice:

And thou must make a dullard of the world,

If they not thought the profits of my death

Were very pregnant and potential spurs

To make thee seek it.'

GLOUCESTER: Strong and fasten'd villain

Would he deny his letter? I never got him.

[*Tucket within*]

Hark, the duke's trumpets! I know not why he

comes.

All ports I'll bar; the villain shall not 'scape;

The duke must grant me that: besides, his

picture

I will send far and near, that all the kingdom

May have the due note of him; and of my land,

Loyal and natural boy, I'll work the means

To make thee capable.

[*Enter CORNWALL, REGAN, and Attendants*]

CORNWALL: How now, my noble friend! since I came hither,

Which I can call but now, I have heard strange news.

REGAN: If it be true, all vengeance comes too short

Which can pursue the offender. How dost, my lord?

GLOUCESTER: O, madam, my old heart is crack'd, it's crack'd!

REGAN: What, did my father's godson seek your life?

He whom my father named? your Edgar?

GLOUCESTER: O, lady, lady, shame would have it hid!

REGAN: Was he not companion with the riotous knights

That tend upon my father?

GLOUCESTER: I know not, madam: 'tis too bad, too bad.

EDMUND: Yes, madam, he was of that consort.

REGAN: No marvel, then, though he were ill affected:

'Tis they have put him on the old man's death,

To have the expense and waste of his revenues.

I have this present evening from my sister

Been well inform'd of them; and with such cautions,

That if they come to sojourn at my house,

I'll not be there.

CORNWALL: Nor I, assure thee, Regan.

Edmund, I hear that you have shown your father

A child-like office.

EDMUND: 'Twas my duty, sir.

GLOUCESTER: He did bewray his practice; and received

This hurt you see, striving to apprehend him.

CORNWALL: Is he pursued?

GLOUCESTER: Ay, my good lord.

CORNWALL: If he be taken, he shall never more

Be fear'd of doing harm: make your own purpose,

How in my strength you please. For you, Edmund,

Whose virtue and obedience doth this instant

So much commend itself, you shall be ours:

Natures of such deep trust we shall much need;

You we first seize on.

EDMUND: I shall serve you, sir,

Truly, however else.

GLOUCESTER: For him I thank your grace.

CORNWALL: You know not why we came to

visit you,–

REGAN: Thus out of season, threading dark-

eyed night:

Occasions, noble Gloucester, of some poise,

Wherein we must have use of your advice:

Our father he hath writ, so hath our sister,

Of differences, which I least thought it fit

To answer from our home; the several

messengers

From hence attend dispatch. Our good old friend,

Lay comforts to your bosom; and bestow

Your needful counsel to our business,

Which craves the instant use.

GLOUCESTER: I serve you, madam:

Your graces are right welcome.

[*Exeunt*]

SCENE II. Before Gloucester's castle.

[*Enter KENT and OSWALD, severally*]

OSWALD: Good dawning to thee, friend: art of this house?

KENT: Ay.

OSWALD: Where may we set our horses?

KENT: I' the mire.

OSWALD: Prithee, if thou lovest me, tell me.

KENT: I love thee not.

OSWALD: Why, then, I care not for thee.

KENT: If I had thee in Lipsbury pinfold, I would make thee care for me.

OSWALD: Why dost thou use me thus? I know thee not.

KENT: Fellow, I know thee.

OSWALD: What dost thou know me for?

KENT: A knave; a rascal; an eater of broken meats; a base, proud, shallow, beggarly, three-suited, hundred-pound, filthy, worsted-stocking knave; a lily-livered, action-taking knave, a whoreson, glass-gazing, super-serviceable finical rogue; one-trunk-inheriting slave; one that wouldst be a bawd, in way of good service, and art nothing but the composition of a knave, beggar, coward, pandar, and the son and heir of a mongrel bitch: one whom I will beat into clamorous whining, if thou deniest the least syllable of thy addition.

OSWALD: Why, what a monstrous fellow art thou, thus to rail on one that is neither known of thee nor knows thee!

KENT: What a brazen-faced varlet art thou, to deny thou knowest me! Is it two days ago since I tripped up thy heels, and beat thee before the king? Draw, you rogue: for, though it be night, yet the moon shines; I'll make a sop o' the moonshine of you: draw, you whoreson cullionly barber-monger, draw.

[*Drawing his sword*]

OSWALD: Away! I have nothing to do with thee.

KENT: Draw, you rascal: you come with letters against the king; and take vanity the puppet's part against the royalty of her father: draw, you rogue, or I'll so carbonado your shanks: draw, you rascal; come your ways.

OSWALD: Help, ho! murder! help!

KENT: Strike, you slave; stand, rogue, stand;

you neat slave, strike.

[*Beating him*]

OSWALD: Help, ho! murder! murder!

[*Enter EDMUND, with his rapier drawn,*
CORNWALL, REGAN, GLOUCESTER, and
Servants]

EDMUND: How now! What's the matter?

[Parting them]

KENT: With you, goodman boy, an you please:
come, I'll flesh ye; come on, young master.

GLOUCESTER: Weapons! arms! What 's the
matter here?

CORNWALL: Keep peace, upon your lives:
He dies that strikes again. What is the matter?

REGAN: The messengers from our sister and
the king.

CORNWALL: What is your difference? speak.

OSWALD: I am scarce in breath, my lord.

KENT: No marvel, you have so bestirred your
valour. You cowardly rascal, nature disclaims in
thee: a tailor made thee.

CORNWALL: Thou art a strange fellow: a tailor
make a man?

KENT: Ay, a tailor, sir: a stone-cutter or painter

could not have made him so ill, though he had
been but two hours at the trade.

CORNWALL: Speak yet, how grew your
quarrel?

OSWALD: This ancient ruffian, sir, whose life I
have spared at suit of his grey beard,—

KENT: Thou whoreson zed! thou unnecessary
letter! My lord, if you will give me leave, I will
tread this unbolted villain into mortar, and daub
the wall of a jakes with him. Spare my grey
beard, you wagtail?

CORNWALL: Peace, sirrah!
You beastly knave, know you no reverence?

KENT: Yes, sir; but anger hath a privilege.

CORNWALL: Why art thou angry?

KENT: That such a slave as this should wear a
sword,
Who wears no honesty. Such smiling rogues as
these,
Like rats, oft bite the holy cords a-twain
Which are too intrinse t' unloose; smooth every
passion
That in the natures of their lords rebel;
Bring oil to fire, snow to their colder moods;

Renege, affirm, and turn their halcyon beaks

With every gale and vary of their masters,

Knowing nought, like dogs, but following.

A plague upon your epileptic visage!

Smile you my speeches, as I were a fool?

Goose, if I had you upon Sarum plain,

I'ld drive ye cackling home to Camelot.

CORNWALL: Why, art thou mad, old fellow?

GLOUCESTER: How fell you out? say that.

KENT: No contraries hold more antipathy

Than I and such a knave.

CORNWALL: Why dost thou call him a knave?

What's his offence?

KENT: His countenance likes me not.

CORNWALL: No more, perchance, does mine,

nor his, nor hers.

KENT: Sir, 'tis my occupation to be plain:

I have seen better faces in my time

Than stands on any shoulder that I see

Before me at this instant.

CORNWALL: This is some fellow,

Who, having been praised for bluntness, doth affect

A saucy roughness, and constrains the garb

Quite from his nature: he cannot flatter, he,

An honest mind and plain, he must speak truth!

An they will take it, so; if not, he's plain.

These kind of knaves I know, which in this

plainness

Harbour more craft and more corrupter ends

Than twenty silly ducking observants

That stretch their duties nicely.

KENT: Sir, in good sooth, in sincere verity,

Under the allowance of your great aspect,

Whose influence, like the wreath of radiant fire

On flickering Phoebus' front,–

CORNWALL: What mean'st by this?

KENT: To go out of my dialect, which you

discommend so much. I know, sir, I am no

flatterer: he that beguiled you in a plain accent

was a plain knave; which for my part I will not be,

though I should win your displeasure to entreat

me to 't.

CORNWALL: What was the offence you gave

him?

OSWALD: I never gave him any:

It pleased the king his master very late

To strike at me, upon his misconstruction;

When he, conjunct and flattering his displeasure,

Tripp'd me behind; being down, insulted, rail'd,

And put upon him such a deal of man,

That worthied him, got praises of the king

For him attempting who was self-subdued;

And, in the fleshment of this dread exploit,

Drew on me here again.

KENT: None of these rogues and cowards

But Ajax is their fool.

CORNWALL: Fetch forth the stocks!

You stubborn ancient knave, you reverend

braggart,

We'll teach you–

KENT: Sir, I am too old to learn:

Call not your stocks for me: I serve the king;

On whose employment I was sent to you:

You shall do small respect, show too bold malice

Against the grace and person of my master,

Stocking his messenger.

CORNWALL: Fetch forth the stocks! As I have

life and honour, There shall he sit till noon.

REGAN: Till noon! till night, my lord; and all night

too.

KENT: Why, madam, if I were your father's dog,

You should not use me so.

REGAN: Sir, being his knave, I will.

CORNWALL: This is a fellow of the self-same colour

Our sister speaks of. Come, bring away the stocks!

[*Stocks brought out*]

GLOUCESTER: Let me beseech your grace not to do so:

His fault is much, and the good king his master

Will cheque him for 't: your purposed low correction

Is such as basest and contemned'st wretches

For pilferings and most common trespasses

Are punish'd with: the king must take it ill,

That he's so slightly valued in his messenger,

Should have him thus restrain'd.

CORNWALL: I'll answer that.

REGAN: My sister may receive it much more worse,

To have her gentleman abused, assaulted,

For following her affairs. Put in his legs.

[*KENT is put in the stocks*]

Come, my good lord, away.

[Exeunt all but GLOUCESTER and KENT]

GLOUCESTER: I am sorry for thee, friend; 'tis the duke's pleasure,

Whose disposition, all the world well knows,

Will not be rubb'd nor stopp'd: I'll entreat for thee.

KENT: Pray, do not, sir: I have watched and travell'd hard;

Some time I shall sleep out, the rest I'll whistle.

A good man's fortune may grow out at heels:

Give you good morrow!

GLOUCESTER: The duke's to blame in this;

'twill be ill taken.

[Exit]

KENT: Good king, that must approve the common saw,

Thou out of heaven's benediction comest

To the warm sun!

Approach, thou beacon to this under globe,

That by thy comfortable beams I may

Peruse this letter! Nothing almost sees miracles

But misery: I know 'tis from Cordelia,

Who hath most fortunately been inform'd

Of my obscured course; and shall find time

From this enormous state, seeking to give

Losses their remedies. All weary and
o'erwatch'd,
Take vantage, heavy eyes, not to behold
This shameful lodging.
Fortune, good night: smile once more: turn thy
wheel!
[*Sleeps*]

SCENE III. Part of the Heath.

[*Enter EDGAR*]
EDGAR: I heard myself proclaim'd;
And by the happy hollow of a tree
Escaped the hunt. No port is free; no place,
That guard, and most unusual vigilance,
Does not attend my taking. Whiles I may 'scape,
I will preserve myself: and am bethought
To take the basest and most poorest shape
That ever penury, in contempt of man,
Brought near to beast: my face I'll grime with filth;
Blanket my loins: elf all my hair in knots;
And with presented nakedness out-face
The winds and persecutions of the sky.
The country gives me proof and precedent

Of Bedlam beggars, who, with roaring voices,

Strike in their numb'd and mortified bare arms

Pins, wooden pricks, nails, sprigs of rosemary;

And with this horrible object, from low farms,

Poor pelting villages, sheep-cotes, and mills,

Sometime with lunatic bans, sometime with
prayers,

Enforce their charity. Poor Turlygood! poor Tom!

That's something yet: Edgar I nothing am.

[*Exit*]

SCENE IV. Before GLOUCESTER's castle.
KENT in the stocks.

[*Enter LEAR, Fool, and Gentleman*]

LEAR: 'Tis strange that they should so depart
from home,

And not send back my messenger.

Gentleman: As I learn'd,

The night before there was no purpose in them

Of this remove.

KENT: Hail to thee, noble master!

LEAR: Ha!

Makest thou this shame thy pastime?

KENT: No, my lord.

Fool: Ha, ha! he wears cruel garters. Horses are tied by the heads, dogs and bears by the neck, monkeys by the loins, and men by the legs: when a man's over-lusty at legs, then he wears wooden nether-stocks.

LEAR: What's he that hath so much thy place mistook

To set thee here?

KENT: It is both he and she;

Your son and daughter.

LEAR: No.

KENT: Yes.

LEAR: No, I say.

KENT: I say, yea.

LEAR: No, no, they would not.

KENT: Yes, they have.

LEAR: By Jupiter, I swear, no.

KENT: By Juno, I swear, ay.

LEAR: They durst not do 't;

They could not, would not do 't; 'tis worse than murder,

To do upon respect such violent outrage:

Resolve me, with all modest haste, which way

Thou mightst deserve, or they impose, this
usage,

Coming from us.

KENT: My lord, when at their home

I did commend your highness' letters to them,

Ere I was risen from the place that show'd

My duty kneeling, came there a reeking post,

Stew'd in his haste, half breathless, panting forth

From Goneril his mistress salutations;

Deliver'd letters, spite of intermission,

Which presently they read: on whose contents,

They summon'd up their meiny, straight took
horse;

Commanded me to follow, and attend

The leisure of their answer; gave me cold looks:

And meeting here the other messenger,

Whose welcome, I perceived, had poison'd
mine,–

Being the very fellow that of late

Display'd so saucily against your highness,–

Having more man than wit about me, drew:

He raised the house with loud and coward cries.

Your son and daughter found this trespass worth

The shame which here it suffers.

Fool: Winter's not gone yet, if the wild-geese fly that way.

Fathers that wear rags

Do make their children blind;

But fathers that bear bags

Shall see their children kind.

Fortune, that arrant whore,

Ne'er turns the key to the poor.

But, for all this, thou shalt have as many dolours for thy daughters as thou canst tell in a year.

LEAR: O, how this mother swells up toward my heart!

Hysterica passio! down, thou climbing sorrow,

Thy element's below! Where is this daughter?

KENT: With the earl, sir, here within.

LEAR: Follow me not;

Stay here.

[*Exit*]

Gentleman: Made you no more offence but what you speak of?

KENT: None.

How chance the king comes with so small a train?

Fool: And thou hadst been set i' the stocks for

that question, thou hadst well deserved it.

KENT: Why, fool?

Fool: We'll set thee to school to an ant, to teach thee there's no labouring i' the winter. All that follow their noses are led by their eyes but blind men; and there's not a nose among twenty but can smell him that's stinking. Let go thy hold when a great wheel runs down a hill, lest it break thy neck with following it: but the great one that goes up the hill, let him draw thee after. When a wise man gives thee better counsel, give me mine again: I would have none but knaves follow it, since a fool gives it.

> That sir which serves and seeks for gain,
> And follows but for form,
> Will pack when it begins to rain,
> And leave thee in the storm,
> But I will tarry; the fool will stay,
> And let the wise man fly:
> The knave turns fool that runs away;
> The fool no knave, perdy.

KENT: Where learned you this, fool?

Fool: Not i' the stocks, fool.

[*Re-enter LEAR with GLOUCESTER*]

LEAR: Deny to speak with me? They are sick?

they are weary?

They have travell'd all the night? Mere fetches;

The images of revolt and flying off.

Fetch me a better answer.

GLOUCESTER: My dear lord,

You know the fiery quality of the duke;

How unremoveable and fix'd he is

In his own course.

LEAR: Vengeance! plague! death! confusion!

Fiery? what quality? Why, Gloucester,

Gloucester,

I'ld speak with the Duke of Cornwall and his wife.

GLOUCESTER: Well, my good lord, I have

inform'd them so.

LEAR: Inform'd them! Dost thou understand me,

man?

GLOUCESTER: Ay, my good lord.

LEAR: The king would speak with Cornwall; the

dear father

Would with his daughter speak, commands her

service:

Are they inform'd of this? My breath and blood!

Fiery? the fiery duke? Tell the hot duke that–

No, but not yet: may be he is not well:

Infirmity doth still neglect all office

Whereto our health is bound; we are not

ourselves

When nature, being oppress'd, commands the

mind

To suffer with the body: I'll forbear;

And am fall'n out with my more headier will,

To take the indisposed and sickly fit

For the sound man. Death on my state!

wherefore

[*Looking on KENT*]

Should he sit here? This act persuades me

That this remotion of the duke and her

Is practice only. Give me my servant forth.

Go tell the duke and 's wife I'ld speak with them,

Now, presently: bid them come forth and hear

me,

Or at their chamber-door I'll beat the drum

Till it cry sleep to death.

GLOUCESTER: I would have all well betwixt

you.

[*Exit*]

LEAR: O me, my heart, my rising heart! but,

down!

Fool: Cry to it, nuncle, as the cockney did to the eels when she put 'em i' the paste alive; she knapped 'em o' the coxcombs with a stick, and cried 'Down, wantons, down!' 'Twas her brother that, in pure kindness to his horse, buttered his hay.

[*Enter CORNWALL, REGAN, GLOUCESTER, and Servants*]

LEAR: Good morrow to you both.

CORNWALL: Hail to your grace!

[*KENT is set at liberty*]

REGAN: I am glad to see your highness.

LEAR: Regan, I think you are; I know what reason

I have to think so: if thou shouldst not be glad,

I would divorce me from thy mother's tomb,

Sepulchring an adultress.

[*To KENT*]

O, are you free?

Some other time for that. Beloved Regan,

Thy sister's naught: O Regan, she hath tied

Sharp-tooth'd unkindness, like a vulture, here:

[*Points to his heart*]

I can scarce speak to thee; thou'lt not believe
With how depraved a quality–O Regan!
REGAN: I pray you, sir, take patience: I have
hope.
You less know how to value her desert
Than she to scant her duty.
LEAR: Say, how is that?
REGAN: I cannot think my sister in the least
Would fail her obligation: if, sir, perchance
She have restrain'd the riots of your followers,
'Tis on such ground, and to such wholesome
end,
As clears her from all blame.
LEAR: My curses on her!
REGAN: O, sir, you are old.
Nature in you stands on the very verge
Of her confine: you should be ruled and led
By some discretion, that discerns your state
Better than you yourself. Therefore, I pray you,
That to our sister you do make return;
Say you have wrong'd her, sir.
LEAR: Ask her forgiveness?
Do you but mark how this becomes the house:
'Dear daughter, I confess that I am old;

[*Kneeling*]

Age is unnecessary: on my knees I beg

That you'll vouchsafe me raiment, bed, and food.'

REGAN: Good sir, no more; these are unsightly tricks:

Return you to my sister.

LEAR: [Rising] Never, Regan:

She hath abated me of half my train;

Look'd black upon me; struck me with her tongue,

Most serpent-like, upon the very heart:

All the stored vengeances of heaven fall

On her ingrateful top! Strike her young bones,

You taking airs, with lameness!

CORNWALL: Fie, sir, fie!

LEAR: You nimble lightnings, dart your blinding flames

Into her scornful eyes! Infect her beauty,

You fen-suck'd fogs, drawn by the powerful sun,

To fall and blast her pride!

REGAN: O, the blest gods! so will you wish on me,

When the rash mood is on.

LEAR: No, Regan, thou shalt never have my

curse:

Thy tender-hefted nature shall not give

Thee o'er to harshness: her eyes are fierce; but
thine

Do comfort and not burn. 'Tis not in thee

To grudge my pleasures, to cut off my train,

To bandy hasty words, to scant my sizes,

And in conclusion to oppose the bolt

Against my coming in: thou better know'st

The offices of nature, bond of childhood,

Effects of courtesy, dues of gratitude;

Thy half o' the kingdom hast thou not forgot,

Wherein I thee endow'd.

REGAN: Good sir, to the purpose.

LEAR: Who put my man i' the stocks?

[*Tucket within*]

CORNWALL: What trumpet's that?

REGAN: I know't, my sister's: this approves her
letter,

That she would soon be here.

[*Enter OSWALD*]

Is your lady come?

LEAR: This is a slave, whose easy-borrow'd
pride

Dwells in the fickle grace of her he follows.

Out, varlet, from my sight!

CORNWALL: What means your grace?

LEAR: Who stock'd my servant? Regan, I have good hope

Thou didst not know on't. Who comes here? O heavens,

[*Enter GONERIL*]

If you do love old men, if your sweet sway

Allow obedience, if yourselves are old,

Make it your cause; send down, and take my part!

[*To GONERIL*]

Art not ashamed to look upon this beard?

O Regan, wilt thou take her by the hand?

GONERIL: Why not by the hand, sir? How have I offended?

All's not offence that indiscretion finds

And dotage terms so.

LEAR: O sides, you are too tough;

Will you yet hold? How came my man i' the stocks?

CORNWALL: I set him there, sir: but his own disorders

Deserved much less advancement.

LEAR: You! did you?

REGAN: I pray you, father, being weak, seem
so.

If, till the expiration of your month,

You will return and sojourn with my sister,

Dismissing half your train, come then to me:

I am now from home, and out of that provision

Which shall be needful for your entertainment.

LEAR: Return to her, and fifty men dismiss'd?

No, rather I abjure all roofs, and choose

To wage against the enmity o' the air;

To be a comrade with the wolf and owl,–

Necessity's sharp pinch! Return with her?

Why, the hot-blooded France, that dowerless
took

Our youngest born, I could as well be brought

To knee his throne, and, squire-like; pension beg

To keep base life afoot. Return with her?

Persuade me rather to be slave and sumpter

To this detested groom.

[*Pointing at OSWALD*]

GONERIL: At your choice, sir.

LEAR: I prithee, daughter, do not make me mad:

I will not trouble thee, my child; farewell:

We'll no more meet, no more see one another:

But yet thou art my flesh, my blood, my daughter;

Or rather a disease that's in my flesh,

Which I must needs call mine: thou art a boil,

A plague-sore, an embossed carbuncle,

In my corrupted blood. But I'll not chide thee;

Let shame come when it will, I do not call it:

I do not bid the thunder-bearer shoot,

Nor tell tales of thee to high-judging Jove:

Mend when thou canst; be better at thy leisure:

I can be patient; I can stay with Regan,

I and my hundred knights.

REGAN: Not altogether so:

I look'd not for you yet, nor am provided

For your fit welcome. Give ear, sir, to my sister;

For those that mingle reason with your passion

Must be content to think you old, and so–

But she knows what she does.

LEAR: Is this well spoken?

REGAN: I dare avouch it, sir: what, fifty

followers?

Is it not well? What should you need of more?

Yea, or so many, sith that both charge and

danger

Speak 'gainst so great a number? How, in one house,

Should many people, under two commands,

Hold amity? 'Tis hard; almost impossible.

GONERIL: Why might not you, my lord, receive attendance

From those that she calls servants or from mine?

REGAN: Why not, my lord? If then they chanced to slack you,

We could control them. If you will come to me,–

For now I spy a danger,–I entreat you

To bring but five and twenty: to no more

Will I give place or notice.

LEAR: I gave you all–

REGAN: And in good time you gave it.

LEAR: Made you my guardians, my depositaries;

But kept a reservation to be follow'd

With such a number. What, must I come to you

With five and twenty, Regan? said you so?

REGAN: And speak't again, my lord; no more with me.

LEAR: Those wicked creatures yet do look well-favour'd,

When others are more wicked: not being the worst

Stands in some rank of praise.

[*To GONERIL*]

I'll go with thee:

Thy fifty yet doth double five and twenty,

And thou art twice her love.

GONERIL: Hear me, my lord;

What need you five and twenty, ten, or five,

To follow in a house where twice so many

Have a command to tend you?

REGAN: What need one?

LEAR: O, reason not the need: our basest beggars

Are in the poorest thing superfluous:

Allow not nature more than nature needs,

Man's life's as cheap as beast's: thou art a lady;

If only to go warm were gorgeous,

Why, nature needs not what thou gorgeous wear'st,

Which scarcely keeps thee warm. But, for true need,—

You heavens, give me that patience, patience I

need!

You see me here, you gods, a poor old man,

As full of grief as age; wretched in both!

If it be you that stir these daughters' hearts

Against their father, fool me not so much

To bear it tamely; touch me with noble anger,

And let not women's weapons, water-drops,

Stain my man's cheeks! No, you unnatural hags,

I will have such revenges on you both,

That all the world shall—I will do such things,—

What they are, yet I know not: but they shall be

The terrors of the earth. You think I'll weep

No, I'll not weep:

I have full cause of weeping; but this heart

Shall break into a hundred thousand flaws,

Or ere I'll weep. O fool, I shall go mad!

[*Exeunt LEAR, GLOUCESTER, KENT, and Fool*]

[*Storm and tempest*]

CORNWALL: Let us withdraw; 'twill be a storm.

REGAN: This house is little: the old man and his people

Cannot be well bestow'd.

GONERIL: 'Tis his own blame; hath put himself from rest,

And must needs taste his folly.

REGAN: For his particular, I'll receive him gladly,

But not one follower.

GONERIL: So am I purposed.

Where is my lord of Gloucester?

CORNWALL: Follow'd the old man forth: he is
return'd.

[*Re-enter GLOUCESTER*]

GLOUCESTER: The king is in high rage.

CORNWALL: Whither is he going?

GLOUCESTER: He calls to horse; but will I know
not whither.

CORNWALL: 'Tis best to give him way; he leads
himself.

GONERIL: My lord, entreat him by no means to
stay.

GLOUCESTER: Alack, the night comes on, and
the bleak winds

Do sorely ruffle; for many miles a bout

There's scarce a bush.

REGAN: O, sir, to wilful men,

The injuries that they themselves procure

Must be their schoolmasters. Shut up your doors:

He is attended with a desperate train;

And what they may incense him to, being apt

To have his ear abused, wisdom bids fear.

CORNWALL: Shut up your doors, my lord; 'tis a

wild night:

My Regan counsels well; come out o' the storm.

[*Exeunt*]

My Notes

ACT III

SCENE I. A heath.

[A *Storm. Enter KENT and a Gentleman, meeting*]

KENT: Who's there, besides foul weather?

Gentleman: One minded like the weather, most unquietly.

KENT: I know you. Where's the king?

Gentleman: Contending with the fretful element:

Bids the winds blow the earth into the sea,

Or swell the curled water 'bove the main,

That things might change or cease; tears his white hair,

Which the impetuous blasts, with eyeless rage,

Catch in their fury, and make nothing of;

Strives in his little world of man to out-scorn

The to-and-fro-conflicting wind and rain.

This night, wherein the cub-drawn bear would couch,

The lion and the belly-pinched wolf

Keep their fur dry, unbonneted he runs,

And bids what will take all.

KENT: But who is with him?

Gentleman: None but the fool; who labours to out-jest

His heart-struck injuries.

KENT: Sir, I do know you;

And dare, upon the warrant of my note,

Commend a dear thing to you. There is division,

Although as yet the face of it be cover'd

With mutual cunning, 'twixt Albany and Cornwall;

Who have—as who have not, that their great stars

Throned and set high?—servants, who seem no less,

Which are to France the spies and speculations

Intelligent of our state; what hath been seen,

Either in snuffs and packings of the dukes,

Or the hard rein which both of them have borne

Against the old kind king; or something deeper,

Whereof perchance these are but furnishings;

But, true it is, from France there comes a power

Into this scatter'd kingdom; who already,

Wise in our negligence, have secret feet

In some of our best ports, and are at point

To show their open banner. Now to you:

If on my credit you dare build so far

To make your speed to Dover, you shall find

Some that will thank you, making just report

Of how unnatural and bemadding sorrow

The king hath cause to plain.

I am a gentleman of blood and breeding;

And, from some knowledge and assurance, offer

This office to you.

Gentleman: I will talk further with you.

KENT: No, do not.

For confirmation that I am much more

Than my out-wall, open this purse, and take

What it contains. If you shall see Cordelia,–

As fear not but you shall,–show her this ring;

And she will tell you who your fellow is

That yet you do not know. Fie on this storm!

I will go seek the king.

Gentleman: Give me your hand: have you no

more to say?

KENT: Few words, but, to effect, more than all

yet;

That, when we have found the king,–in which

your pain

That way, I'll this,–he that first lights on him

Holla the other.   [*Exeunt severally*]

SCENE II. Another part of the heath. Storm still.

[*Enter LEAR and Fool*]

LEAR: Blow, winds, and crack your cheeks! rage! blow!

You cataracts and hurricanoes, spout

Till you have drench'd our steeples, drown'd the cocks!

You sulphurous and thought-executing fires,

Vaunt-couriers to oak-cleaving thunderbolts,

Singe my white head! And thou, all-shaking thunder,

Smite flat the thick rotundity o' the world!

Crack nature's moulds, an germens spill at once,

That make ingrateful man!

Fool: O nuncle, court holy-water in a dry house is better than this rain-water out o' door. Good nuncle, in, and ask thy daughters' blessing: here's a night pities neither wise man nor fool.

LEAR: Rumble thy bellyful! Spit, fire! spout, rain!

Nor rain, wind, thunder, fire, are my daughters:

I tax not you, you elements, with unkindness;

I never gave you kingdom, call'd you children,

You owe me no subscription: then let fall

Your horrible pleasure: here I stand, your slave,

A poor, infirm, weak, and despised old man:

But yet I call you servile ministers,

That have with two pernicious daughters join'd

Your high engender'd battles 'gainst a head

So old and white as this. O! O! 'tis foul!

Fool: He that has a house to put's head in has a good head-piece.

The cod-piece that will house

Before the head has any,

The head and he shall louse;

So beggars marry many.

The man that makes his toe

What he his heart should make

Shall of a corn cry woe,

And turn his sleep to wake.

For there was never yet fair woman but she made mouths in a glass.

LEAR: No, I will be the pattern of all patience;

I will say nothing.

[*Enter KENT*]

KENT: Who's there?

Fool: Marry, here's grace and a cod-piece; that's a wise man and a fool.

KENT: Alas, sir, are you here? things that love night
Love not such nights as these; the wrathful skies
Gallow the very wanderers of the dark,
And make them keep their caves: since I was man,
Such sheets of fire, such bursts of horrid thunder,
Such groans of roaring wind and rain, I never
Remember to have heard: man's nature cannot carry
The affliction nor the fear.

LEAR: Let the great gods,
That keep this dreadful pother o'er our heads,
Find out their enemies now. Tremble, thou wretch,
That hast within thee undivulged crimes,
Unwhipp'd of justice: hide thee, thou bloody hand;
Thou perjured, and thou simular man of virtue
That art incestuous: caitiff, to pieces shake,
That under covert and convenient seeming

Hast practiced on man's life: close pent-up guilts,

Rive your concealing continents, and cry

These dreadful summoners grace. I am a man

More sinn'd against than sinning.

KENT: Alack, bare-headed!

Gracious my lord, hard by here is a hovel;

Some friendship will it lend you 'gainst the

tempest:

Repose you there; while I to this hard house—

More harder than the stones whereof 'tis raised;

Which even but now, demanding after you,

Denied me to come in—return, and force

Their scanted courtesy.

LEAR: My wits begin to turn.

Come on, my boy: how dost, my boy? art cold?

I am cold myself. Where is this straw, my fellow?

The art of our necessities is strange,

That can make vile things precious. Come, your

hovel.

Poor fool and knave, I have one part in my heart

That's sorry yet for thee.

Fool: [Singing]

He that has and a little tiny wit—

With hey, ho, the wind and the rain,—

Must make content with his fortunes fit,

For the rain it raineth every day.

LEAR: True, my good boy. Come, bring us to this hovel.

[*Exeunt LEAR and KENT*]

Fool: This is a brave night to cool a courtezan. I'll speak a prophecy ere I go:

When priests are more in word than matter;

When brewers mar their malt with water;

When nobles are their tailors' tutors;

No heretics burn'd, but wenches' suitors;

When every case in law is right;

No squire in debt, nor no poor knight;

When slanders do not live in tongues;

Nor cutpurses come not to throngs;

When usurers tell their gold i' the field;

And bawds and whores do churches build;

Then shall the realm of Albion

Come to great confusion:

Then comes the time, who lives to see't,

That going shall be used with feet.

This prophecy Merlin shall make; for I live before his time.   [*Exit*]

SCENE III. A Room in Gloucester's castle.

[*Enter GLOUCESTER and EDMUND*]

GLOUCESTER: Alack, alack, Edmund, I like not this unnatural dealing. When I desire their leave that I might pity him, they took from me the use of mine own house; charged me, on pain of their perpetual displeasure, neither to speak of him, entreat for him, nor any way sustain him.

EDMUND: Most savage and unnatural!

GLOUCESTER: Go to; say you nothing. There's a division betwixt the dukes; and a worse matter than that: I have received a letter this night; 'tis dangerous to be spoken; I have locked the letter in my closet: these injuries the king now bears will be revenged home; there's part of a power already footed: we must incline to the king. I will seek him, and privily relieve him: go you and maintain talk with the duke, that my charity be not of him perceived: if he ask for me. I am ill, and gone to bed. Though I die for it, as no less is threatened me, the king my old master must be relieved. There is some strange thing toward, Edmund; pray you, be careful.

[*Exit*]

EDMUND: This courtesy, forbid thee, shall the duke

Instantly know; and of that letter too:

This seems a fair deserving, and must draw me

That which my father loses; no less than all:

The younger rises when the old doth fall.

[*Exit*]

SCENE IV. The heath. Before a hovel.

[*Enter LEAR, KENT, and Fool*]

KENT: Here is the place, my lord; good my lord, enter:

The tyranny of the open night's too rough

For nature to endure.

[*Storm still*]

LEAR: Let me alone.

KENT: Good my lord, enter here.

LEAR: Wilt break my heart?

KENT: I had rather break mine own. Good my lord, enter.

LEAR: Thou think'st 'tis much that this contentious storm

Invades us to the skin: so 'tis to thee;

But where the greater malady is fix'd,

The lesser is scarce felt. Thou'ldst shun a bear;

But if thy flight lay toward the raging sea,

Thou'ldst meet the bear i' the mouth. When the

mind's free,

The body's delicate: the tempest in my mind

Doth from my senses take all feeling else

Save what beats there. Filial ingratitude!

Is it not as this mouth should tear this hand

For lifting food to't? But I will punish home:

No, I will weep no more. In such a night

To shut me out! Pour on; I will endure.

In such a night as this! O Regan, Goneril!

Your old kind father, whose frank heart gave all,—

O, that way madness lies; let me shun that;

No more of that.

KENT: Good my lord, enter here.

LEAR: Prithee, go in thyself: seek thine own

ease:

This tempest will not give me leave to ponder

On things would hurt me more. But I'll go in.

[*To the Fool*]

In, boy; go first. You houseless poverty,—

Nay, get thee in. I'll pray, and then I'll sleep.

[*Fool goes in*]

Poor naked wretches, whereso'er you are,

That bide the pelting of this pitiless storm,

How shall your houseless heads and unfed

sides,

Your loop'd and window'd raggedness, defend

you

From seasons such as these? O, I have ta'en

Too little care of this! Take physic, pomp;

Expose thyself to feel what wretches feel,

That thou mayst shake the superflux to them,

And show the heavens more just.

EDGAR: [Within] Fathom and half, fathom and

half! Poor Tom!

[*The Fool runs out from the hovel*]

Fool: Come not in here, nuncle, here's a spirit.

Help me, help me!

KENT: Give me thy hand. Who's there?

Fool: A spirit, a spirit: he says his name's poor

Tom.

KENT: What art thou that dost grumble there i'

the straw?

Come forth.

[*Enter EDGAR disguised as a mad man*]

EDGAR: Away! the foul fiend follows me!

Through the sharp hawthorn blows the cold wind.

Hum! go to thy cold bed, and warm thee.

LEAR: Hast thou given all to thy two daughters?

And art thou come to this?

EDGAR: Who gives any thing to poor Tom?

whom the foul fiend hath led through fire and

through flame, and through ford and whirlpool

e'er bog and quagmire; that hath laid knives

under his pillow, and halters in his pew; set

ratsbane by his porridge; made film proud of

heart, to ride on a bay trotting-horse over four-

inched bridges, to course his own shadow for a

traitor. Bless thy five wits! Tom's a-cold. O, do

de, do de, do de. Bless thee from whirlwinds,

star-blasting, and taking! Do poor Tom some

charity, whom the foul fiend vexes: there could I

have him now, and there, and there again, and

there.

[*Storm still*]

LEAR: What, have his daughters brought him to

this pass?

Couldst thou save nothing? Didst thou give them

all?

Fool: Nay, he reserved a blanket, else we had been all shamed.

LEAR: Now, all the plagues that in the pendulous air

Hang fated o'er men's faults light on thy daughters!

KENT: He hath no daughters, sir.

LEAR: Death, traitor! nothing could have subdued nature

To such a lowness but his unkind daughters.

Is it the fashion, that discarded fathers

Should have thus little mercy on their flesh?

Judicious punishment! 'twas this flesh begot

Those pelican daughters.

EDGAR: Pillicock sat on Pillicock-hill:

Halloo, halloo, loo, loo!

Fool: This cold night will turn us all to fools and madmen.

EDGAR: Take heed o' the foul fiend: obey thy parents; keep thy word justly; swear not; commit not with man's sworn spouse; set not thy sweet heart on proud array. Tom's a-cold.

LEAR: What hast thou been?

EDGAR: A serving-man, proud in heart and mind; that curled my hair; wore gloves in my cap; served the lust of my mistress' heart, and did the act of darkness with her; swore as many oaths as I spake words, and broke them in the sweet face of heaven: one that slept in the contriving of lust, and waked to do it: wine loved I deeply, dice dearly: and in woman out-paramoured the Turk: false of heart, light of ear, bloody of hand; hog in sloth, fox in stealth, wolf in greediness, dog in madness, lion in prey. Let not the creaking of shoes nor the rustling of silks betray thy poor heart to woman: keep thy foot out of brothels, thy hand out of plackets, thy pen from lenders' books, and defy the foul fiend. Still through the hawthorn blows the cold wind: Says suum, mun, ha, no, nonny. Dolphin my boy, my boy, sessa! let him trot by.

[*Storm still*]

LEAR: Why, thou wert better in thy grave than to answer with thy uncovered body this extremity of the skies. Is man no more than this? Consider him well. Thou owest the worm no silk, the beast no hide, the sheep no wool, the cat no perfume.

Ha! here's three on 's are sophisticated! Thou art the thing itself: unaccommodated man is no more but such a poor bare, forked animal as thou art. Off, off, you lendings! come unbutton here.

[*Tearing off his clothes*]

Fool: Prithee, nuncle, be contented; 'tis a naughty night to swim in. Now a little fire in a wild field were like an old lecher's heart; a small spark, all the rest on's body cold. Look, here comes a walking fire.

[*Enter GLOUCESTER, with a torch*]

EDGAR: This is the foul fiend Flibbertigibbet: he begins at curfew, and walks till the first cock; he gives the web and the pin, squints the eye, and makes the hare-lip; mildews the white wheat, and hurts the poor creature of earth.

　　Swithold footed thrice the old;

　　He met the night-mare, and her nine-fold;

　　Bid her alight,

　　And her troth plight,

　　And, aroint thee, witch, aroint thee!

KENT: How fares your grace?

LEAR: What's he?

KENT: Who's there? What is't you seek?

GLOUCESTER: What are you there? Your names?

EDGAR: Poor Tom; that eats the swimming frog, the toad, the tadpole, the wall-newt and the water; that in the fury of his heart, when the foul fiend rages, eats cow-dung for sallets; swallows the old rat and the ditch-dog; drinks the green mantle of the standing pool; who is whipped from tithing to tithing, and stock- punished, and imprisoned; who hath had three suits to his back, six shirts to his body, horse to ride, and weapon to wear;

But mice and rats, and such small deer,

Have been Tom's food for seven long year.

Beware my follower. Peace, Smulkin; peace, thou fiend!

GLOUCESTER: What, hath your grace no better company?

EDGAR: The prince of darkness is a gentleman: Modo he's call'd, and Mahu.

GLOUCESTER: Our flesh and blood is grown so vile, my lord,

That it doth hate what gets it.

EDGAR: Poor Tom's a-cold.

GLOUCESTER: Go in with me: my duty cannot suffer

To obey in all your daughters' hard commands:

Though their injunction be to bar my doors,

And let this tyrannous night take hold upon you,

Yet have I ventured to come seek you out,

And bring you where both fire and food is ready.

LEAR: First let me talk with this philosopher.

What is the cause of thunder?

KENT: Good my lord, take his offer; go into the house.

LEAR: I'll talk a word with this same learned Theban.

What is your study?

EDGAR: How to prevent the fiend, and to kill vermin.

LEAR: Let me ask you one word in private.

KENT: Importune him once more to go, my lord; His wits begin to unsettle.

GLOUCESTER: Canst thou blame him?

[*Storm still*]

His daughters seek his death: ah, that good Kent!

He said it would be thus, poor banish'd man!

Thou say'st the king grows mad; I'll tell thee, friend,

I am almost mad myself: I had a son,

Now outlaw'd from my blood; he sought my life,

But lately, very late: I loved him, friend;

No father his son dearer: truth to tell thee,

The grief hath crazed my wits. What a night's this!

I do beseech your grace,–

LEAR: O, cry your mercy, sir.

Noble philosopher, your company.

EDGAR: Tom's a-cold.

GLOUCESTER: In, fellow, there, into the hovel: keep thee warm.

LEAR: Come let's in all.

KENT: This way, my lord.

LEAR: With him;

I will keep still with my philosopher.

KENT: Good my lord, soothe him; let him take the fellow.

GLOUCESTER: Take him you on.

KENT: Sirrah, come on; go along with us.

LEAR: Come, good Athenian.

GLOUCESTER: No words, no words: hush.

EDGAR: Child Rowland to the dark tower came,

His word was still,–Fie, foh, and fum,

I smell the blood of a British man.

[*Exeunt*]

SCENE V. A Room in Gloucester's castle.

[*Enter CORNWALL and EDMUND*]

CORNWALL: I will have my revenge ere I depart his house.

EDMUND: How, my lord, I may be censured, that nature thus gives way to loyalty, something fears me to think of.

CORNWALL: I now perceive, it was not altogether your brother's evil disposition made him seek his death; but a provoking merit, set a-work by a reprovable badness in himself.

EDMUND: How malicious is my fortune, that I must repent to be just! This is the letter he spoke of, which approves him an intelligent party to the advantages of France: O heavens! that this treason were not, or not I the detector!

CORNWALL: Go with me to the duchess.

EDMUND: If the matter of this paper be certain, you have mighty business in hand.

CORNWALL: True or false, it hath made thee earl of Gloucester. Seek out where thy father is, that he may be ready for our apprehension.

EDMUND: [Aside] If I find him comforting the king, it will stuff his suspicion more fully.—I will persevere in my course of loyalty, though the conflict be sore between that and my blood.

CORNWALL: I will lay trust upon thee; and thou shalt find a dearer father in my love.

[*Exeunt*]

SCENE VI. A chamber in a farmhouse adjoining the castle.

[*Enter GLOUCESTER, LEAR, KENT, Fool, and EDGAR*]

GLOUCESTER: Here is better than the open air; take it thankfully. I will piece out the comfort with what addition I can: I will not be long from you.

KENT: All the power of his wits have given way to his impatience: the gods reward your kindness!

[*Exit GLOUCESTER*]

EDGAR: Frateretto calls me; and tells me
Nero is an angler in the lake of darkness.
Pray, innocent, and beware the foul fiend.

Fool: Prithee, nuncle, tell me whether a madman
be a gentleman or a yeoman?

LEAR: A king, a king!

Fool: No, he's a yeoman that has a gentleman to
his son; for he's a mad yeoman that sees his son
a gentleman before him.

LEAR: To have a thousand with red burning
spits
Come hissing in upon 'em,–

EDGAR: The foul fiend bites my back.

Fool: He's mad that trusts in the tameness of a
wolf, a horse's health, a boy's love, or a whore's
oath.

LEAR: It shall be done; I will arraign them
straight.

[*To EDGAR*]

Come, sit thou here, most learned justicer;

[*To the Fool*]

Thou, sapient sir, sit here. Now, you she foxes!

EDGAR: Look, where he stands and glares!

Wantest thou eyes at trial, madam?

Come o'er the bourn, Bessy, to me,–

Fool: Her boat hath a leak,

And she must not speak

Why she dares not come over to thee.

EDGAR: The foul fiend haunts poor Tom in the voice of a nightingale. Hopdance cries in Tom's belly for two white herring. Croak not, black angel; I have no food for thee.

KENT: How do you, sir? Stand you not so amazed:

Will you lie down and rest upon the cushions?

LEAR: I'll see their trial first. Bring in the evidence.

[*To EDGAR*]

Thou robed man of justice, take thy place;

[*To the Fool*]

And thou, his yoke-fellow of equity,

Bench by his side:

[*To KENT*]

you are o' the commission,

Sit you too.

EDGAR: Let us deal justly.

   Sleepest or wakest thou, jolly shepherd?

Thy sheep be in the corn;

And for one blast of thy minikin mouth,

Thy sheep shall take no harm.

Purr! the cat is grey.

LEAR: Arraign her first; 'tis Goneril. I here take my oath before this honourable assembly, she kicked the poor king her father.

Fool: Come hither, mistress. Is your name Goneril?

LEAR: She cannot deny it.

Fool: Cry you mercy, I took you for a joint-stool.

LEAR: And here's another, whose warp'd looks proclaim

What store her heart is made on. Stop her there!

Arms, arms, sword, fire! Corruption in the place!

False justicer, why hast thou let her 'scape?

EDGAR: Bless thy five wits!

KENT: O pity! Sir, where is the patience now,

That thou so oft have boasted to retain?

EDGAR: [Aside] My tears begin to take his part so much,

They'll mar my counterfeiting.

LEAR: The little dogs and all,

Tray, Blanch, and Sweet-heart, see, they bark at

me.

EDGAR: Tom will throw his head at them.

Avaunt, you curs!

  Be thy mouth or black or white,

  Tooth that poisons if it bite;

  Mastiff, grey-hound, mongrel grim,

  Hound or spaniel, brach or lym,

  Or bobtail tike or trundle-tail,

  Tom will make them weep and wail:

  For, with throwing thus my head,

  Dogs leap the hatch, and all are fled.

Do de, de, de. Sessa! Come, march to wakes
and

fairs and market-towns. Poor Tom, thy horn is
dry.

LEAR: Then let them anatomize Regan; see
what breeds about her heart. Is there any cause
in nature that makes these hard hearts?

[*To EDGAR*]

You, sir, I entertain for one of my hundred; only I
do not like the fashion of your garments: you will
say they are Persian attire: but let them be
changed.

KENT: Now, good my lord, lie here and rest

awhile.

LEAR: Make no noise, make no noise; draw the curtains: so, so, so. We'll go to supper i' he morning. So, so, so.

Fool: And I'll go to bed at noon.

[*Re-enter GLOUCESTER*]

GLOUCESTER: Come hither, friend: where is the king my master?

KENT: Here, sir; but trouble him not, his wits are gone.

GLOUCESTER: Good friend, I prithee, take him in thy arms;

I have o'erheard a plot of death upon him:

There is a litter ready; lay him in 't,

And drive towards Dover, friend, where thou shalt meet

Both welcome and protection. Take up thy master:

If thou shouldst dally half an hour, his life,

With thine, and all that offer to defend him,

Stand in assured loss: take up, take up;

And follow me, that will to some provision

Give thee quick conduct.

KENT: Oppressed nature sleeps:

This rest might yet have balm'd thy broken senses,

Which, if convenience will not allow,

Stand in hard cure.

[*To the Fool*]

Come, help to bear thy master;

Thou must not stay behind.

GLOUCESTER: Come, come, away.

[*Exeunt all but EDGAR*]

EDGAR: When we our betters see bearing our woes,

We scarcely think our miseries our foes.

Who alone suffers suffers most i' the mind,

Leaving free things and happy shows behind:

But then the mind much sufferance doth o'er skip,

When grief hath mates, and bearing fellowship.

How light and portable my pain seems now,

When that which makes me bend makes the king bow,

He childed as I father'd! Tom, away!

Mark the high noises; and thyself bewray,

When false opinion, whose wrong thought defiles thee,

In thy just proof, repeals and reconciles thee.

What will hap more to-night, safe 'scape the king!

Lurk, lurk.

[*Exit*]

SCENE VII. A Room in Gloucester's castle.

[*Enter CORNWALL, REGAN, GONERIL,*
EDMUND, and Servants]

CORNWALL: Post speedily to my lord your
husband; show him this letter: the army of
France is landed. Seek out the villain Gloucester.

[*Exeunt some of the Servants*]

REGAN: Hang him instantly.

GONERIL: Pluck out his eyes.

CORNWALL: Leave him to my displeasure.
Edmund, keep you our sister company: the
revenges we are bound to take upon your
traitorous father are not fit for your beholding.
Advise the duke, where you are going, to a most
festinate preparation: we are bound to the like.
Our posts shall be swift and intelligent betwixt us.
Farewell, dear sister: farewell, my lord of
Gloucester.

[*Enter OSWALD*]

How now! where's the king?

OSWALD: My lord of Gloucester hath convey'd
him hence:

Some five or six and thirty of his knights,

Hot questrists after him, met him at gate;

Who, with some other of the lords dependants,

Are gone with him towards Dover; where they
boast

To have well-armed friends.

CORNWALL: Get horses for your mistress.

GONERIL: Farewell, sweet lord, and sister.

CORNWALL: Edmund, farewell.

[*Exeunt GONERIL, EDMUND, and OSWALD*]

Go seek the traitor Gloucester,

Pinion him like a thief, bring him before us.

[*Exeunt other Servants*]

Though well we may not pass upon his life

Without the form of justice, yet our power

Shall do a courtesy to our wrath, which men

May blame, but not control. Who's there? the
traitor?

[*Enter GLOUCESTER, brought in by two or
three*]

REGAN: Ingrateful fox! 'tis he.

CORNWALL: Bind fast his corky arms.

GLOUCESTER: What mean your graces? Good my friends, consider
You are my guests: do me no foul play, friends.

CORNWALL: Bind him, I say.

[*Servants bind him*]

REGAN: Hard, hard. O filthy traitor!

GLOUCESTER: Unmerciful lady as you are, I'm none.

CORNWALL: To this chair bind him. Villain, thou shalt find–

[*REGAN plucks his beard*]

GLOUCESTER: By the kind gods, 'tis most ignobly done
To pluck me by the beard.

REGAN: So white, and such a traitor!

GLOUCESTER: Naughty lady,
These hairs, which thou dost ravish from my chin,
Will quicken, and accuse thee: I am your host:
With robbers' hands my hospitable favours
You should not ruffle thus. What will you do?

CORNWALL: Come, sir, what letters had you

late from France?

REGAN: Be simple answerer, for we know the truth.

CORNWALL: And what confederacy have you with the traitors
Late footed in the kingdom?

REGAN: To whose hands have you sent the lunatic king? Speak.

GLOUCESTER: I have a letter guessingly set down,
Which came from one that's of a neutral heart,
And not from one opposed.

CORNWALL: Cunning.

REGAN: And false.

CORNWALL: Where hast thou sent the king?

GLOUCESTER: To Dover.

REGAN: Wherefore to Dover? Wast thou not charged at peril—

CORNWALL: Wherefore to Dover? Let him first answer that.

GLOUCESTER: I am tied to the stake, and I must stand the course.

REGAN: Wherefore to Dover, sir?

GLOUCESTER: Because I would not see thy

cruel nails

Pluck out his poor old eyes; nor thy fierce sister

In his anointed flesh stick boarish fangs.

The sea, with such a storm as his bare head

In hell-black night endured, would have buoy'd

up,

And quench'd the stelled fires:

Yet, poor old heart, he holp the heavens to rain.

If wolves had at thy gate howl'd that stern time,

Thou shouldst have said 'Good porter, turn the

key,'

All cruels else subscribed: but I shall see

The winged vengeance overtake such children.

CORNWALL: See't shalt thou never. Fellows,

hold the chair.

Upon these eyes of thine I'll set my foot.

GLOUCESTER: He that will think to live till he be

old,

Give me some help! O cruel! O you gods!

REGAN: One side will mock another; the other

too.

CORNWALL: If you see vengeance,–

First Servant: Hold your hand, my lord:

I have served you ever since I was a child;

But better service have I never done you

Than now to bid you hold.

REGAN: How now, you dog!

First Servant: If you did wear a beard upon your
chin,

I'd shake it on this quarrel. What do you mean?

CORNWALL: My villain!

[*They draw and fight*]

First Servant: Nay, then, come on, and take the
chance of anger.

REGAN: Give me thy sword. A peasant stand up
thus!

[*Takes a sword, and runs at him behind*]

First Servant: O, I am slain! My lord, you have
one eye left

To see some mischief on him. O!

[*Dies*]

CORNWALL: Lest it see more, prevent it. Out,
vile jelly!

Where is thy lustre now?

GLOUCESTER: All dark and comfortless.

Where's my son Edmund?

Edmund, enkindle all the sparks of nature,

To quit this horrid act.

REGAN: Out, treacherous villain!

Thou call'st on him that hates thee: it was he

That made the overture of thy treasons to us;

Who is too good to pity thee.

GLOUCESTER: O my follies! then Edgar was abused.

Kind gods, forgive me that, and prosper him!

REGAN: Go thrust him out at gates, and let him smell

His way to Dover.

[*Exit one with GLOUCESTER*]

How is't, my lord? how look you?

CORNWALL: I have received a hurt: follow me, lady.

Turn out that eyeless villain; throw this slave

Upon the dunghill. Regan, I bleed apace:

Untimely comes this hurt: give me your arm.

[*Exit CORNWALL, led by REGAN*]

Second Servant: I'll never care what wickedness I do,

If this man come to good.

Third Servant: If she live long,

And in the end meet the old course of death,

Women will all turn monsters.

Second Servant: Let's follow the old earl, and get the Bedlam

To lead him where he would: his roguish madness

Allows itself to any thing.

Third Servant: Go thou: I'll fetch some flax and whites of eggs

To apply to his bleeding face. Now, heaven help him!

[*Exeunt severally*]

My Notes

ACT IV

SCENE I. The heath.

[*Enter EDGAR*]

EDGAR: Yet better thus, and known to be contemn'd,

Than still contemn'd and flatter'd. To be worst,

The lowest and most dejected thing of fortune,

Stands still in esperance, lives not in fear:

The lamentable change is from the best;

The worst returns to laughter. Welcome, then,

Thou unsubstantial air that I embrace!

The wretch that thou hast blown unto the worst

Owes nothing to thy blasts. But who comes here?

[*Enter GLOUCESTER, led by an Old Man*]

My father, poorly led? World, world, O world!

But that thy strange mutations make us hate thee,

Lie would not yield to age.

Old Man: O, my good lord, I have been your tenant, and your father's tenant, these fourscore years.

141

GLOUCESTER: Away, get thee away; good friend, be gone:

Thy comforts can do me no good at all;

Thee they may hurt.

Old Man: Alack, sir, you cannot see your way.

GLOUCESTER: I have no way, and therefore want no eyes;

I stumbled when I saw: full oft 'tis seen,

Our means secure us, and our mere defects

Prove our commodities. O dear son Edgar,

The food of thy abused father's wrath!

Might I but live to see thee in my touch,

I'ld say I had eyes again!

Old Man: How now! Who's there?

EDGAR: [Aside] O gods! Who is't can say 'I am at the worst'?

I am worse than e'er I was.

Old Man: 'Tis poor mad Tom.

EDGAR: [Aside] And worse I may be yet: the worst is not

So long as we can say 'This is the worst.'

Old Man: Fellow, where goest?

GLOUCESTER: Is it a beggar-man?

Old Man: Madman and beggar too.

GLOUCESTER: He has some reason, else he could not beg.

I' the last night's storm I such a fellow saw;

Which made me think a man a worm: my son

Came then into my mind; and yet my mind

Was then scarce friends with him: I have heard more since.

As flies to wanton boys, are we to the gods.

They kill us for their sport.

EDGAR: [Aside] How should this be?

Bad is the trade that must play fool to sorrow,

Angering itself and others.–Bless thee, master!

GLOUCESTER: Is that the naked fellow?

Old Man: Ay, my lord.

GLOUCESTER: Then, prithee, get thee gone: if, for my sake,

Thou wilt o'ertake us, hence a mile or twain,

I' the way toward Dover, do it for ancient love;

And bring some covering for this naked soul,

Who I'll entreat to lead me.

Old Man: Alack, sir, he is mad.

GLOUCESTER: 'Tis the times' plague, when madmen lead the blind.

Do as I bid thee, or rather do thy pleasure;

Above the rest, be gone.

Old Man: I'll bring him the best 'parel that I have,

Come on't what will.

[*Exit*]

GLOUCESTER: Sirrah, naked fellow,–

EDGAR: Poor Tom's a-cold.

[*Aside*]

I cannot daub it further.

GLOUCESTER: Come hither, fellow.

EDGAR: [Aside] And yet I must.–Bless thy sweet

eyes, they bleed.

GLOUCESTER: Know'st thou the way to Dover?

EDGAR: Both stile and gate, horse-way and

foot-path. Poor Tom hath been scared out of his

good wits: bless thee, good man's son, from the

foul fiend! Five fiends have been in poor Tom at

once; of lust, as Obidicut; Hobbididence, prince

of dumbness; Mahu, of stealing; Modo, of

murder; Flibbertigibbet, of mopping and mowing,

who since possesses chambermaids and

waiting-women. So, bless thee, master!

GLOUCESTER: Here, take this purse, thou

whom the heavens' plagues

Have humbled to all strokes: that I am wretched

Makes thee the happier: heavens, deal so still!

Let the superfluous and lust-dieted man,

That slaves your ordinance, that will not see

Because he doth not feel, feel your power

quickly;

So distribution should undo excess,

And each man have enough. Dost thou know

Dover?

EDGAR: Ay, master.

GLOUCESTER: There is a cliff, whose high and

bending head

Looks fearfully in the confined deep:

Bring me but to the very brim of it,

And I'll repair the misery thou dost bear

With something rich about me: from that place

I shall no leading need.

EDGAR: Give me thy arm:

Poor Tom shall lead thee.

[*Exeunt*]

SCENE II. Before ALBANY's palace.

[*Enter GONERIL and EDMUND*]

GONERIL: Welcome, my lord: I marvel our mild

husband

Not met us on the way.

[*Enter OSWALD*]

Now, where's your master?

OSWALD: Madam, within; but never man so changed.

I told him of the army that was landed;

He smiled at it: I told him you were coming:

His answer was 'The worse:' of Gloucester's treachery,

And of the loyal service of his son,

When I inform'd him, then he call'd me sot,

And told me I had turn'd the wrong side out:

What most he should dislike seems pleasant to him;

What like, offensive.

GONERIL: [To EDMUND] Then shall you go no further.

It is the cowish terror of his spirit,

That dares not undertake: he'll not feel wrongs

Which tie him to an answer. Our wishes on the way

May prove effects. Back, Edmund, to my brother;

Hasten his musters and conduct his powers:

I must change arms at home, and give the distaff

Into my husband's hands. This trusty servant

Shall pass between us: ere long you are like to

hear,

If you dare venture in your own behalf,

A mistress's command. Wear this; spare speech;

[*Giving a favour*]

Decline your head: this kiss, if it durst speak,

Would stretch thy spirits up into the air:

Conceive, and fare thee well.

EDMUND: Yours in the ranks of death.

GONERIL: My most dear Gloucester!

[*Exit EDMUND*]

O, the difference of man and man!

To thee a woman's services are due:

My fool usurps my body.

OSWALD: Madam, here comes my lord.

[*Exit*]

[*Enter ALBANY*]

GONERIL: I have been worth the whistle.

ALBANY: O Goneril!

You are not worth the dust which the rude wind

Blows in your face. I fear your disposition:

That nature, which contemns its origin,

Cannot be border'd certain in itself;

She that herself will sliver and disbranch

From her material sap, perforce must wither

And come to deadly use.

GONERIL: No more; the text is foolish.

ALBANY: Wisdom and goodness to the vile

seem vile:

Filths savour but themselves. What have you

done?

Tigers, not daughters, what have you perform'd?

A father, and a gracious aged man,

Whose reverence even the head-lugg'd bear

would lick,

Most barbarous, most degenerate! have you

madded.

Could my good brother suffer you to do it?

A man, a prince, by him so benefited!

If that the heavens do not their visible spirits

Send quickly down to tame these vile offences,

It will come,

Humanity must perforce prey on itself,

Like monsters of the deep.

GONERIL: Milk-liver'd man!

That bear'st a cheek for blows, a head for

wrongs;

Who hast not in thy brows an eye discerning

Thine honour from thy suffering; that not know'st

Fools do those villains pity who are punish'd

Ere they have done their mischief. Where's thy
drum?

France spreads his banners in our noiseless
land;

With plumed helm thy slayer begins threats;

Whiles thou, a moral fool, sit'st still, and criest

'Alack, why does he so?'

ALBANY: See thyself, devil!

Proper deformity seems not in the fiend

So horrid as in woman.

GONERIL: O vain fool!

ALBANY: Thou changed and self-cover'd thing,
for shame,

Be-monster not thy feature. Were't my fitness

To let these hands obey my blood,

They are apt enough to dislocate and tear

Thy flesh and bones: howe'er thou art a fiend,

A woman's shape doth shield thee.

GONERIL: Marry, your manhood now–

[*Enter a Messenger*]

ALBANY: What news?

Messenger: O, my good lord, the Duke of
Cornwall's dead:
Slain by his servant, going to put out
The other eye of Gloucester.

ALBANY: Gloucester's eye!

Messenger: A servant that he bred, thrill'd with
remorse,
Opposed against the act, bending his sword
To his great master; who, thereat enraged,
Flew on him, and amongst them fell'd him dead;
But not without that harmful stroke, which since
Hath pluck'd him after.

ALBANY: This shows you are above,
You justicers, that these our nether crimes
So speedily can venge! But, O poor Gloucester!
Lost he his other eye?

Messenger: Both, both, my lord.
This letter, madam, craves a speedy answer;
'Tis from your sister.

GONERIL: [Aside] One way I like this well;
But being widow, and my Gloucester with her,
May all the building in my fancy pluck
Upon my hateful life: another way,

150

The news is not so tart.–I'll read, and answer.

[*Exit*]

ALBANY: Where was his son when they did
take his eyes?

Messenger: Come with my lady hither.

ALBANY: He is not here.

Messenger: No, my good lord; I met him back
again.

ALBANY: Knows he the wickedness?

Messenger: Ay, my good lord; 'twas he inform'd
against him;

And quit the house on purpose, that their
punishment

Might have the freer course.

ALBANY: Gloucester, I live

To thank thee for the love thou show'dst the king,

And to revenge thine eyes. Come hither, friend:

Tell me what more thou know'st.

[*Exeunt*]

SCENE III. The French camp near Dover.

[*Enter KENT and a Gentleman*]

KENT: Why the King of France is so suddenly

gone back know you the reason?

Gentleman: Something he left imperfect in the state, which since his coming forth is thought of; which imports to the kingdom so much fear and danger, that his personal return was most required and necessary.

KENT: Who hath he left behind him general?

Gentleman: The Marshal of France, Monsieur la Far.

KENT: Did your letters pierce the queen to any demonstration of grief?

Gentleman: Ay, sir; she took them, read them in my presence;

And now and then an ample tear trill'd down

Her delicate cheek: it seem'd she was a queen

Over her passion; who, most rebel-like,

Sought to be king o'er her.

KENT: O, then it moved her.

Gentleman: Not to a rage: patience and sorrow strove

Who should express her goodliest. You have seen

Sunshine and rain at once: her smiles and tears

Were like a better way: those happy smilets,

That play'd on her ripe lip, seem'd not to know

What guests were in her eyes; which parted thence,

As pearls from diamonds dropp'd. In brief,

Sorrow would be a rarity most beloved,

If all could so become it.

KENT: Made she no verbal question?

Gentleman: 'Faith, once or twice she heaved the name of 'father'

Pantingly forth, as if it press'd her heart:

Cried 'Sisters! sisters! Shame of ladies! sisters!

Kent! father! sisters! What, i' the storm? i' the night?

Let pity not be believed!' There she shook

The holy water from her heavenly eyes,

And clamour moisten'd: then away she started

To deal with grief alone.

KENT: It is the stars,

The stars above us, govern our conditions;

Else one self mate and mate could not beget

Such different issues. You spoke not with her since?

Gentleman: No.

KENT: Was this before the king return'd?

Gentleman: No, since.

KENT: Well, sir, the poor distressed Lear's i' the town;

Who sometime, in his better tune, remembers

What we are come about, and by no means

Will yield to see his daughter.

Gentleman: Why, good sir?

KENT: A sovereign shame so elbows him: his own unkindness,

That stripp'd her from his benediction, turn'd her

To foreign casualties, gave her dear rights

To his dog-hearted daughters, these things sting

His mind so venomously, that burning shame

Detains him from Cordelia.

Gentleman: Alack, poor gentleman!

KENT: Of Albany's and Cornwall's powers you heard not?

Gentleman: 'Tis so, they are afoot.

KENT: Well, sir, I'll bring you to our master Lear,

And leave you to attend him: some dear cause

Will in concealment wrap me up awhile;

When I am known aright, you shall not grieve

Lending me this acquaintance. I pray you, go

Along with me.   [*Exeunt*]

SCENE IV. The same. A tent.

[*Enter, with drum and colours, CORDELIA, Doctor, and Soldiers*]

CORDELIA: Alack, 'tis he: why, he was met even now

As mad as the vex'd sea; singing aloud;

Crown'd with rank fumiter and furrow-weeds,

With bur-docks, hemlock, nettles, cuckoo-flowers,

Darnel, and all the idle weeds that grow

In our sustaining corn. A century send forth;

Search every acre in the high-grown field,

And bring him to our eye.

[*Exit an Officer*]

What can man's wisdom

In the restoring his bereaved sense?

He that helps him take all my outward worth.

Doctor: There is means, madam:

Our foster-nurse of nature is repose,

The which he lacks; that to provoke in him,

Are many simples operative, whose power

Will close the eye of anguish.

CORDELIA: All blest secrets,

All you unpublish'd virtues of the earth,

Spring with my tears! be aidant and remediate

In the good man's distress! Seek, seek for him;

Lest his ungovern'd rage dissolve the life

That wants the means to lead it.

[*Enter a Messenger*]

Messenger: News, madam;

The British powers are marching hitherward.

CORDELIA: 'Tis known before; our preparation

stands

In expectation of them. O dear father,

It is thy business that I go about;

Therefore great France

My mourning and important tears hath pitied.

No blown ambition doth our arms incite,

But love, dear love, and our aged father's right:

Soon may I hear and see him!

[*Exeunt*]

SCENE V. A Room in Gloucester's castle.

[*Enter REGAN and OSWALD*]

REGAN: But are my brother's powers set forth?

OSWALD: Ay, madam.

REGAN: Himself in person there?

OSWALD: Madam, with much ado:

Your sister is the better soldier.

REGAN: Lord Edmund spake not with your lord at home?

OSWALD: No, madam.

REGAN: What might import my sister's letter to him?

OSWALD: I know not, lady.

REGAN: 'Faith, he is posted hence on serious matter.

It was great ignorance, Gloucester's eyes being out,

To let him live: where he arrives he moves

All hearts against us: Edmund, I think, is gone,

In pity of his misery, to dispatch

His nighted life: moreover, to descry

The strength o' the enemy.

OSWALD: I must needs after him, madam, with my letter.

REGAN: Our troops set forth to-morrow: stay with us;

The ways are dangerous.

OSWALD: I may not, madam:

My lady charged my duty in this business.

REGAN: Why should she write to Edmund?
Might not you
Transport her purposes by word? Belike,
Something–I know not what: I'll love thee much,
Let me unseal the letter.

OSWALD: Madam, I had rather–

REGAN: I know your lady does not love her
husband;
I am sure of that: and at her late being here
She gave strange oeillades and most speaking
looks
To noble Edmund. I know you are of her bosom.

OSWALD: I, madam?

REGAN: I speak in understanding; you are; I
know't:
Therefore I do advise you, take this note:
My lord is dead; Edmund and I have talk'd;
And more convenient is he for my hand
Than for your lady's: you may gather more.
If you do find him, pray you, give him this;
And when your mistress hears thus much from
you,
I pray, desire her call her wisdom to her.

So, fare you well.

If you do chance to hear of that blind traitor,

Preferment falls on him that cuts him off.

OSWALD: Would I could meet him, madam! I should show

What party I do follow.

REGAN: Fare thee well.

[*Exeunt*]

SCENE VI. The Country near Dover.

[*Enter GLOUCESTER, and EDGAR dressed like a peasant*]

GLOUCESTER: When shall we come to the top of that same hill?

EDGAR: You do climb up it now: look, how we labour.

GLOUCESTER: Methinks the ground is even.

EDGAR: Horrible steep.

Hark, do you hear the sea?

GLOUCESTER: No, truly.

EDGAR: Why, then, your other senses grow imperfect

By your eyes' anguish.

GLOUCESTER: So may it be, indeed:

Methinks thy voice is alter'd; and thou speak'st

In better phrase and matter than thou didst.

EDGAR: You're much deceived: in nothing am I changed

But in my garments.

GLOUCESTER: Methinks you're better spoken.

EDGAR: Come on, sir; here's the place: stand still. How fearful

And dizzy 'tis, to cast one's eyes so low!

The crows and choughs that wing the midway air

Show scarce so gross as beetles: half way down

Hangs one that gathers samphire, dreadful trade!

Methinks he seems no bigger than his head:

The fishermen, that walk upon the beach,

Appear like mice; and yond tall anchoring bark,

Diminish'd to her cock; her cock, a buoy

Almost too small for sight: the murmuring surge,

That on the unnumber'd idle pebbles chafes,

Cannot be heard so high. I'll look no more;

Lest my brain turn, and the deficient sight

Topple down headlong.

GLOUCESTER: Set me where you stand.

EDGAR: Give me your hand: you are now within

a foot

Of the extreme verge: for all beneath the moon

Would I not leap upright.

GLOUCESTER: Let go my hand.

Here, friend, 's another purse; in it a jewel

Well worth a poor man's taking: fairies and gods

Prosper it with thee! Go thou farther off;

Bid me farewell, and let me hear thee going.

EDGAR: Now fare you well, good sir.

GLOUCESTER: With all my heart.

EDGAR: Why I do trifle thus with his despair

Is done to cure it.

GLOUCESTER: [Kneeling] O you mighty gods!

This world I do renounce, and, in your sights,

Shake patiently my great affliction off:

If I could bear it longer, and not fall

To quarrel with your great opposeless wills,

My snuff and loathed part of nature should

Burn itself out. If Edgar live, O, bless him!

Now, fellow, fare thee well.

[*He falls forward*]

EDGAR: Gone, sir: farewell.

And yet I know not how conceit may rob

The treasury of life, when life itself

Yields to the theft: had he been where he thought,

By this, had thought been past. Alive or dead?

Ho, you sir! friend! Hear you, sir! speak!

Thus might he pass indeed: yet he revives.

What are you, sir?

GLOUCESTER: Away, and let me die.

EDGAR: Hadst thou been aught but gossamer, feathers, air,

So many fathom down precipitating,

Thou'dst shiver'd like an egg: but thou dost breathe;

Hast heavy substance; bleed'st not; speak'st; art sound.

Ten masts at each make not the altitude

Which thou hast perpendicularly fell:

Thy life's a miracle. Speak yet again.

GLOUCESTER: But have I fall'n, or no?

EDGAR: From the dread summit of this chalky bourn.

Look up a-height; the shrill-gorged lark so far

Cannot be seen or heard: do but look up.

GLOUCESTER: Alack, I have no eyes.

Is wretchedness deprived that benefit,

To end itself by death? 'Twas yet some comfort,

When misery could beguile the tyrant's rage,

And frustrate his proud will.

EDGAR: Give me your arm:

Up: so. How is 't? Feel you your legs? You stand.

GLOUCESTER: Too well, too well.

EDGAR: This is above all strangeness.

Upon the crown o' the cliff, what thing was that

Which parted from you?

GLOUCESTER: A poor unfortunate beggar.

EDGAR: As I stood here below, methought his

eyes

Were two full moons; he had a thousand noses,

Horns whelk'd and waved like the enridged sea:

It was some fiend; therefore, thou happy father,

Think that the clearest gods, who make them

honours

Of men's impossibilities, have preserved thee.

GLOUCESTER: I do remember now: henceforth

I'll bear

Affliction till it do cry out itself

'Enough, enough,' and die. That thing you speak

of,

I took it for a man; often 'twould say

'The fiend, the fiend:' he led me to that place.

EDGAR: Bear free and patient thoughts. But who comes here?

[*Enter LEAR, fantastically dressed with wild flowers*]

The safer sense will ne'er accommodate His master thus.

LEAR: No, they cannot touch me for coining; I am the king himself.

EDGAR: O thou side-piercing sight!

LEAR: Nature's above art in that respect. There's your press-money. That fellow handles his bow like a crow-keeper: draw me a clothier's yard. Look, look, a mouse! Peace, peace; this piece of toasted cheese will do 't. There's my gauntlet; I'll prove it on a giant. Bring up the brown bills. O, well flown, bird! i' the clout, i' the clout: hewgh! Give the word.

EDGAR: Sweet marjoram.

LEAR: Pass.

GLOUCESTER: I know that voice.

LEAR: Ha! Goneril, with a white beard! They flattered me like a dog; and told me I had white hairs in my beard ere the black ones were there.

To say 'ay' and 'no' to every thing that I said!–'Ay' and 'no' too was no good divinity. When the rain came to wet me once, and the wind to make me chatter; when the thunder would not peace at my bidding; there I found 'em, there I smelt 'em out. Go to, they are not men o' their words: they told me I was every thing; 'tis a lie, I am not ague-proof.

GLOUCESTER: The trick of that voice I do well remember:

Is 't not the king?

LEAR: Ay, every inch a king:

When I do stare, see how the subject quakes.

I pardon that man's life. What was thy cause?

Adultery?

Thou shalt not die: die for adultery! No:

The wren goes to 't, and the small gilded fly

Does lecher in my sight.

Let copulation thrive; for Gloucester's bastard

son

Was kinder to his father than my daughters

Got 'tween the lawful sheets.

To 't, luxury, pell-mell! for I lack soldiers.

Behold yond simpering dame,

Whose face between her forks presages snow;

That minces virtue, and does shake the head

To hear of pleasure's name;

The fitchew, nor the soiled horse, goes to 't

With a more riotous appetite.

Down from the waist they are Centaurs,

Though women all above:

But to the girdle do the gods inherit,

Beneath is all the fiends';

There's hell, there's darkness, there's the

sulphurous pit,

Burning, scalding, stench, consumption; fie, fie,

fie! pah, pah! Give me an ounce of civet, good

apothecary, to sweeten my imagination: there's

money for thee.

GLOUCESTER: O, let me kiss that hand!

LEAR: Let me wipe it first; it smells of mortality.

GLOUCESTER: O ruin'd piece of nature! This

great world

Shall so wear out to nought. Dost thou know me?

LEAR: I remember thine eyes well enough. Dost

thou squiny at me? No, do thy worst, blind Cupid!

I'll not love. Read thou this challenge; mark but

the penning of it.

GLOUCESTER: Were all the letters suns, I could not see one.

EDGAR: I would not take this from report; it is, And my heart breaks at it.

LEAR: Read.

GLOUCESTER: What, with the case of eyes?

LEAR: O, ho, are you there with me? No eyes in your head, nor no money in your purse? Your eyes are in a heavy case, your purse in a light; yet you see how this world goes.

GLOUCESTER: I see it feelingly.

LEAR: What, art mad? A man may see how this world goes with no eyes. Look with thine ears: see how yond justice rails upon yond simple thief. Hark, in thine ear: change places; and, handy-dandy, which is the justice, which is the thief? Thou hast seen a farmer's dog bark at a beggar?

GLOUCESTER: Ay, sir.

LEAR: And the creature run from the cur? There thou mightst behold the great image of authority: a dog's obeyed in office.
Thou rascal beadle, hold thy bloody hand!
Why dost thou lash that whore? Strip thine own

back;

Thou hotly lust'st to use her in that kind

For which thou whipp'st her. The usurer hangs

the cozener.

Through tatter'd clothes small vices do appear;

Robes and furr'd gowns hide all. Plate sin with

gold,

And the strong lance of justice hurtless breaks:

Arm it in rags, a pigmy's straw does pierce it.

None does offend, none, I say, none; I'll able

'em:

Take that of me, my friend, who have the power

To seal the accuser's lips. Get thee glass eyes;

And like a scurvy politician, seem

To see the things thou dost not. Now, now, now,

now:

Pull off my boots: harder, harder: so.

EDGAR: O, matter and impertinency mix'd!

Reason in madness!

LEAR: If thou wilt weep my fortunes, take my

eyes.

I know thee well enough; thy name is Gloucester:

Thou must be patient; we came crying hither:

Thou know'st, the first time that we smell the air,

We wawl and cry. I will preach to thee: mark.

GLOUCESTER: Alack, alack the day!

LEAR: When we are born, we cry that we are come

To this great stage of fools: this a good block;

It were a delicate stratagem, to shoe

A troop of horse with felt: I'll put 't in proof;

And when I have stol'n upon these sons-in-law,

Then, kill, kill, kill, kill, kill, kill!

[*Enter a Gentleman, with Attendants*]

Gentleman: O, here he is: lay hand upon him. Sir,

Your most dear daughter–

LEAR: No rescue? What, a prisoner? I am even

The natural fool of fortune. Use me well;

You shall have ransom. Let me have surgeons;

I am cut to the brains.

Gentleman: You shall have any thing.

LEAR: No seconds? all myself?

Why, this would make a man a man of salt,

To use his eyes for garden water-pots,

Ay, and laying autumn's dust.

Gentleman: Good sir,–

LEAR: I will die bravely, like a bridegroom. What!

I will be jovial: come, come; I am a king,

My masters, know you that.

Gentleman: You are a royal one, and we obey
you.

LEAR: Then there's life in't. Nay, if you get it,
you

shall get it with running. Sa, sa, sa, sa.

[*Exit. Attendants follow*]

Gentleman: A sight most pitiful in the meanest
wretch,

Past speaking of in a king! Thou hast one
daughter,

Who redeems nature from the general curse

Which twain have brought her to.

EDGAR: Hail, gentle sir.

Gentleman: Sir, speed you: what's your will?

EDGAR: Do you hear aught, sir, of a battle
toward?

Gentleman: Most sure and vulgar: every one
hears that,

Which can distinguish sound.

EDGAR: But, by your favour,

How near's the other army?

Gentleman: Near and on speedy foot; the main

descry

Stands on the hourly thought.

EDGAR: I thank you, sir: that's all.

Gentleman: Though that the queen on special
cause is here,

Her army is moved on.

EDGAR: I thank you, sir.

[*Exit Gentleman*]

GLOUCESTER: You ever-gentle gods, take my
breath from me:

Let not my worser spirit tempt me again

To die before you please!

EDGAR: Well pray you, father.

GLOUCESTER: Now, good sir, what are you?

EDGAR: A most poor man, made tame to
fortune's blows;

Who, by the art of known and feeling sorrows,

Am pregnant to good pity. Give me your hand,

I'll lead you to some biding.

GLOUCESTER: Hearty thanks:

The bounty and the benison of heaven

To boot, and boot!

[*Enter OSWALD*]

OSWALD: A proclaim'd prize! Most happy!

That eyeless head of thine was first framed flesh

To raise my fortunes. Thou old unhappy traitor,

Briefly thyself remember: the sword is out

That must destroy thee.

GLOUCESTER: Now let thy friendly hand

Put strength enough to't.

[*EDGAR interposes*]

OSWALD: Wherefore, bold peasant,

Darest thou support a publish'd traitor? Hence;

Lest that the infection of his fortune take

Like hold on thee. Let go his arm.

EDGAR: Ch'ill not let go, zir, without vurther

'casion.

OSWALD: Let go, slave, or thou diest!

EDGAR: Good gentleman, go your gait, and let

poor volk pass. An chud ha' bin zwaggered out of

my life, 'twould not ha' bin zo long as 'tis by a

vortnight. Nay, come not near th' old man; keep

out, che vor ye, or ise try whether your costard or

my ballow be the harder: ch'ill be plain with you.

OSWALD: Out, dunghill!

EDGAR: Ch'ill pick your teeth, zir: come; no

matter vor your foins.

[*They fight, and EDGAR knocks him down*]

OSWALD: Slave, thou hast slain me: villain, take

my purse:

If ever thou wilt thrive, bury my body;

And give the letters which thou find'st about me

To Edmund earl of Gloucester; seek him out

Upon the English party: O, untimely death!

[*Dies*]

EDGAR: I know thee well: a serviceable villain;

As duteous to the vices of thy mistress

As badness would desire.

GLOUCESTER: What, is he dead?

EDGAR: Sit you down, father; rest you

Let's see these pockets: the letters that he

speaks of

May be my friends. He's dead; I am only sorry

He had no other death's-man. Let us see:

Leave, gentle wax; and, manners, blame us not:

To know our enemies' minds, we'ld rip their

hearts;

Their papers, is more lawful.

[*Reads*]

'Let our reciprocal vows be remembered. You

have many opportunities to cut him off: if your

will want not, time and place will be fruitfully

offered. There is nothing done, if he return the
conqueror: then am I the prisoner, and his bed
my goal; from the loathed warmth whereof
deliver me, and supply the place for your labour.
'Your—wife, so I would say—
'Affectionate servant,
'GONERIL.'
O undistinguish'd space of woman's will!
A plot upon her virtuous husband's life;
And the exchange my brother! Here, in the
sands,
Thee I'll rake up, the post unsanctified
Of murderous lechers: and in the mature time
With this ungracious paper strike the sight
Of the death practiced duke: for him 'tis well
That of thy death and business I can tell.
GLOUCESTER; The king is mad: how stiff is my
vile sense,
That I stand up, and have ingenious feeling
Of my huge sorrows! Better I were distract:
So should my thoughts be sever'd from my
griefs,
And woes by wrong imaginations lose
The knowledge of themselves.

EDGAR: Give me your hand:

[*Drum afar off*]

Far off, methinks, I hear the beaten drum:

Come, father, I'll bestow you with a friend.

[*Exeunt*]

SCENE VII. A tent in the French camp.

[*Enter CORDELIA, KENT, Doctor and Gentleman*]

CORDELIA: O thou good Kent, how shall I live and work,

To match thy goodness? My life will be too short,

And every measure fail me.

KENT: To be acknowledged, madam, is o'erpaid.

All my reports go with the modest truth;

Nor more nor clipp'd, but so.

CORDELIA: Be better suited:

These weeds are memories of those worser hours:

I prithee, put them off.

KENT: Pardon me, dear madam;

Yet to be known shortens my made intent:

My boon I make it, that you know me not

Till time and I think meet.

CORDELIA: Then be't so, my good lord.

[*To the Doctor*]

How does the king?

Doctor: Madam, sleeps still.

CORDELIA: O you kind gods,

Cure this great breach in his abused nature!

The untuned and jarring senses, O, wind up

Of this child-changed father!

Doctor: So please your majesty

That we may wake the king: he hath slept long.

CORDELIA: Be govern'd by your knowledge, and proceed

I' the sway of your own will. Is he array'd?

[Enter LEAR in his chair, carried by Servants]

Gentleman: Ay, madam; in the heaviness of his sleep

We put fresh garments on him.

Doctor: Be by, good madam, when we do awake him;

I doubt not of his temperance.

CORDELIA: Very well.

Doctor: Please you, draw near. Louder the music there!

CORDELIA: O my dear father! Restoration hang

Thy medicine on my lips; and let this kiss

Repair those violent harms that my two sisters

Have in thy reverence made!

KENT: Kind and dear princess!

CORDELIA: Had you not been their father, these white flakes

Had challenged pity of them. Was this a face

To be opposed against the warring winds?

To stand against the deep dread-bolted thunder?

In the most terrible and nimble stroke

Of quick, cross lightning? to watch–poor perdu!–

With this thin helm? Mine enemy's dog,

Though he had bit me, should have stood that night

Against my fire; and wast thou fain, poor father,

To hovel thee with swine, and rogues forlorn,

In short and musty straw? Alack, alack!

'Tis wonder that thy life and wits at once

Had not concluded all. He wakes; speak to him.

Doctor: Madam, do you; 'tis fittest.

CORDELIA: How does my royal lord? How fares your majesty?

LEAR: You do me wrong to take me out o' the

grave:

Thou art a soul in bliss; but I am bound

Upon a wheel of fire, that mine own tears

Do scald like molten lead.

CORDELIA: Sir, do you know me?

LEAR: You are a spirit, I know: when did you die?

CORDELIA: Still, still, far wide!

Doctor: He's scarce awake: let him alone awhile.

LEAR: Where have I been? Where am I? Fair daylight?

I am mightily abused. I should e'en die with pity,

To see another thus. I know not what to say.

I will not swear these are my hands: let's see;

I feel this pin prick. Would I were assured

Of my condition!

CORDELIA: O, look upon me, sir,

And hold your hands in benediction o'er me:

No, sir, you must not kneel.

LEAR: Pray, do not mock me:

I am a very foolish fond old man,

Fourscore and upward, not an hour more nor less;

And, to deal plainly,

I fear I am not in my perfect mind.

Methinks I should know you, and know this man;

Yet I am doubtful for I am mainly ignorant

What place this is; and all the skill I have

Remembers not these garments; nor I know not

Where I did lodge last night. Do not laugh at me;

For, as I am a man, I think this lady

To be my child Cordelia.

CORDELIA: And so I am, I am.

LEAR: Be your tears wet? yes, 'faith. I pray, weep not:

If you have poison for me, I will drink it.

I know you do not love me; for your sisters

Have, as I do remember, done me wrong:

You have some cause, they have not.

CORDELIA: No cause, no cause.

LEAR: Am I in France?

KENT: In your own kingdom, sir.

LEAR: Do not abuse me.

Doctor: Be comforted, good madam: the great rage,

You see, is kill'd in him: and yet it is danger

To make him even o'er the time he has lost.

Desire him to go in; trouble him no more

Till further settling.

CORDELIA: Will't please your highness walk?

LEAR: You must bear with me:

Pray you now, forget and forgive: I am old and

foolish.

[Exeunt all but KENT and Gentleman]

Gentleman: Holds it true, sir, that the Duke of

Cornwall was so slain?

KENT: Most certain, sir.

Gentleman: Who is conductor of his people?

KENT: As 'tis said, the bastard son of

Gloucester.

Gentleman: They say Edgar, his banished son,

is with the Earl of Kent in Germany.

KENT: Report is changeable. 'Tis time to look

about; the powers of the kingdom approach

apace.

Gentleman: The arbitrement is like to be bloody.

Fare you well, sir.

[Exit]

KENT: My point and period will be throughly

wrought,

Or well or ill, as this day's battle's fought.

[Exit]

My Notes

ACT V

SCENE I. The British camp, near Dover.

[*Enter, with drum and colours, EDMUND,
REGAN, Officers, Soldiers and Others.*]

EDMUND: Know of the duke if his last purpose
hold,

Or whether since he is advised by aught

To change the course: he's full of alteration

And self-reproving: bring his constant pleasure.

[*To an Officer, who goes out*]

REGAN: Our sister's man is certainly miscarried.

EDMUND: 'Tis to be doubted, madam.

REGAN: Now, sweet lord,

You know the goodness I intend upon you:

Tell me—but truly—but then speak the truth,

Do you not love my sister?

EDMUND: In honour'd love.

REGAN: But have you never found my brother's
way

To the forfended place?

EDMUND: That thought abuses you.

REGAN: I am doubtful that you have been

conjunct

And bosom'd with her, as far as we call hers.

EDMUND: No, by mine honour, madam.

REGAN: I never shall endure her: dear my lord,

Be not familiar with her.

EDMUND: Fear me not:

She and the duke her husband!

[*Enter, with drum and colours, ALBANY,*

GONERIL, and Soldiers]

GONERIL: [Aside] I had rather lose the battle

than that sister

Should loosen him and me.

ALBANY: Our very loving sister, well be-met.

Sir, this I hear; the king is come to his daughter,

With others whom the rigor of our state

Forced to cry out. Where I could not be honest,

I never yet was valiant: for this business,

It toucheth us, as France invades our land,

Not bolds the king, with others, whom, I fear,

Most just and heavy causes make oppose.

EDMUND: Sir, you speak nobly.

REGAN: Why is this reason'd?

GONERIL: Combine together 'gainst the enemy;

For these domestic and particular broils

Are not the question here.

ALBANY: Let's then determine

With the ancient of war on our proceedings.

EDMUND: I shall attend you presently at your

tent.

REGAN: Sister, you'll go with us?

GONERIL: No.

REGAN: 'Tis most convenient; pray you, go with

us.

GONERIL: [Aside] O, ho, I know the riddle.–I will

go.

[*As they are going out, enter EDGAR disguised*]

EDGAR: If e'er your grace had speech with man

so poor,

Hear me one word.

ALBANY: I'll overtake you. Speak.

[*Exeunt all but ALBANY and EDGAR*]

EDGAR: Before you fight the battle, ope this

letter.

If you have victory, let the trumpet sound

For him that brought it: wretched though I seem,

I can produce a champion that will prove

What is avouched there. If you miscarry,

Your business of the world hath so an end,

And machination ceases. Fortune love you.

ALBANY: Stay till I have read the letter.

EDGAR: I was forbid it.

When time shall serve, let but the herald cry,

And I'll appear again.

ALBANY: Why, fare thee well: I will o'erlook thy

paper.

[*Exit EDGAR*]

[*Re-enter EDMUND*]

EDMUND: The enemy's in view; draw up your

powers.

Here is the guess of their true strength and

forces

By diligent discovery; but your haste

Is now urged on you.

ALBANY: We will greet the time.

[*Exit*]

EDMUND: To both these sisters have I sworn

my love;

Each jealous of the other, as the stung

Are of the adder. Which of them shall I take?

Both? one? or neither? Neither can be enjoy'd,

If both remain alive: to take the widow

Exasperates, makes mad her sister Goneril;

And hardly shall I carry out my side,

Her husband being alive. Now then we'll use

His countenance for the battle; which being

done,

Let her who would be rid of him devise

His speedy taking off. As for the mercy

Which he intends to Lear and to Cordelia,

The battle done, and they within our power,

Shall never see his pardon; for my state

Stands on me to defend, not to debate.

[*Exit*]

SCENE II. A field between the two camps.

[*Alarum within. Enter, with drum and colours,
LEAR, CORDELIA, and Soldiers, and exeunt*]

[*Enter EDGAR and GLOUCESTER*]

EDGAR: Here, father, take the shadow of this
tree

For your good host; pray that the right may
thrive:

If ever I return to you again,

I'll bring you comfort.

GLOUCESTER: Grace go with you, sir!

[*Exit EDGAR*]

[*Alarum and retreat within. Re-enter EDGAR*]

EDGAR: Away, old man; give me thy hand;
away!

King Lear hath lost, he and his daughter ta'en:
Give me thy hand; come on.

GLOUCESTER: No farther, sir; a man may rot
even here.

EDGAR: What, in ill thoughts again? Men must
endure

Their going hence, even as their coming hither;
Ripeness is all: come on.

GLOUCESTER: And that's true too.

[*Exeunt*]

SCENE III. The British camp near Dover.

[*Enter, in conquest, with drum and colours,
EDMUND, LEAR and CORDELIA, prisoners;
Officers, Soldiers, etc*]

EDMUND: Some officers take them away: good
guard,

Until their greater pleasures first be known
That are to censure them.

CORDELIA: We are not the first

Who, with best meaning, have incurr'd the worst.

For thee, oppressed king, am I cast down;

Myself could else out-frown false fortune's frown.

Shall we not see these daughters and these

sisters?

LEAR: No, no, no, no! Come, let's away to

prison:

We two alone will sing like birds i' the cage:

When thou dost ask me blessing, I'll kneel down,

And ask of thee forgiveness: so we'll live,

And pray, and sing, and tell old tales, and laugh

At gilded butterflies, and hear poor rogues

Talk of court news; and we'll talk with them too,

Who loses and who wins; who's in, who's out;

And take upon's the mystery of things,

As if we were God's spies: and we'll wear out,

In a wall'd prison, packs and sects of great ones,

That ebb and flow by the moon.

EDMUND: Take them away.

LEAR: Upon such sacrifices, my Cordelia,

The gods themselves throw incense. Have I

caught thee?

He that parts us shall bring a brand from heaven,

And fire us hence like foxes. Wipe thine eyes;

The good-years shall devour them, flesh and fell,

Ere they shall make us weep: we'll see 'em

starve first. Come.

[*Exeunt LEAR and CORDELIA, guarded*]

EDMUND: Come hither, captain; hark.

Take thou this note;

[*Giving a paper*]

go follow them to prison:

One step I have advanced thee; if thou dost

As this instructs thee, thou dost make thy way

To noble fortunes: know thou this, that men

Are as the time is: to be tender-minded

Does not become a sword: thy great employment

Will not bear question; either say thou'lt do 't,

Or thrive by other means.

Officer: I'll do 't, my lord.

EDMUND: About it; and write happy when thou

hast done.

Mark, I say, instantly; and carry it so

As I have set it down.

Officer: I cannot draw a cart, nor eat dried oats;

If it be man's work, I'll do 't.

[*Exit*]

[*Flourish. Enter ALBANY, GONERIL, REGAN, Officers, and Soldiers*]

ALBANY: Sir, you have shown to-day your valiant strain,

And fortune led you well: you have the captives

That were the opposites of this day's strife:

We do require them of you, so to use them

As we shall find their merits and our safety

May equally determine.

EDMUND: Sir, I thought it fit

To send the old and miserable king

To some retention and appointed guard;

Whose age has charms in it, whose title more,

To pluck the common bosom on his side,

An turn our impress'd lances in our eyes

Which do command them. With him I sent the queen;

My reason all the same; and they are ready

To-morrow, or at further space, to appear

Where you shall hold your session. At this time

We sweat and bleed: the friend hath lost his friend;

And the best quarrels, in the heat, are cursed

By those that feel their sharpness:

The question of Cordelia and her father

Requires a fitter place.

ALBANY: Sir, by your patience,

I hold you but a subject of this war,

Not as a brother.

REGAN: That's as we list to grace him.

Methinks our pleasure might have been demanded,

Ere you had spoke so far. He led our powers;

Bore the commission of my place and person;

The which immediacy may well stand up,

And call itself your brother.

GONERIL: Not so hot:

In his own grace he doth exalt himself,

More than in your addition.

REGAN: In my rights,

By me invested, he compeers the best.

GONERIL: That were the most, if he should husband you.

REGAN: Jesters do oft prove prophets.

GONERIL: Holla, holla!

That eye that told you so look'd but a-squint.

REGAN: Lady, I am not well; else I should answer

From a full-flowing stomach. General,

Take thou my soldiers, prisoners, patrimony;

Dispose of them, of me; the walls are thine:

Witness the world, that I create thee here

My lord and master.

GONERIL: Mean you to enjoy him?

ALBANY: The let-alone lies not in your good will.

EDMUND: Nor in thine, lord.

ALBANY: Half-blooded fellow, yes.

REGAN: [To EDMUND] Let the drum strike, and

prove my title thine.

ALBANY: Stay yet; hear reason. Edmund, I

arrest thee

On capital treason; and, in thine attaint,

This gilded serpent

[*Pointing to Goneril*]

For your claim, fair sister,

I bar it in the interest of my wife:

'Tis she is sub-contracted to this lord,

And I, her husband, contradict your bans.

If you will marry, make your loves to me,

My lady is bespoke.

GONERIL: An interlude!

ALBANY: Thou art arm'd, Gloucester: let the

trumpet sound:

If none appear to prove upon thy head

Thy heinous, manifest, and many treasons,

There is my pledge;

[*Throwing down a glove*]

I'll prove it on thy heart,

Ere I taste bread, thou art in nothing less

Than I have here proclaim'd thee.

REGAN: Sick, O, sick!

GONERIL: [Aside] If not, I'll ne'er trust medicine.

EDMUND: There's my exchange:

[*Throwing down a glove*]

what in the world he is

That names me traitor, villain-like he lies:

Call by thy trumpet: he that dares approach,

On him, on you, who not? I will maintain

My truth and honour firmly.

ALBANY: A herald, ho!

EDMUND: A herald, ho, a herald!

ALBANY: Trust to thy single virtue; for thy

soldiers,

All levied in my name, have in my name

Took their discharge.

REGAN: My sickness grows upon me.

ALBANY: She is not well; convey her to my tent.

[*Exit Regan, led*]

[*Enter a Herald*]

Come hither, herald,–Let the trumpet sound,

And read out this.

Officer: Sound, trumpet!

[*A trumpet sounds*]

Herald: [Reads] *'If any man of quality or degree within the lists of the army will maintain upon Edmund, supposed Earl of Gloucester, that he is a manifold traitor, let him appear by the third sound of the trumpet: he is bold in his defence.'*

EDMUND: Sound!

[*First trumpet*]

Herald: Again!

[*Second trumpet*]

Herald: Again!

[*Third trumpet*]

[*Trumpet answers within*]

[*Enter EDGAR, at the third sound, armed, with a trumpet before him*]

ALBANY: Ask him his purposes, why he appears

Upon this call o' the trumpet.

Herald: What are you?

Your name, your quality? and why you answer

This present summons?

EDGAR: Know, my name is lost;

By treason's tooth bare-gnawn and canker-bit:

Yet am I noble as the adversary

I come to cope.

ALBANY: Which is that adversary?

EDGAR: What's he that speaks for Edmund Earl

of Gloucester?

EDMUND: Himself: what say'st thou to him?

EDGAR: Draw thy sword,

That, if my speech offend a noble heart,

Thy arm may do thee justice: here is mine.

Behold, it is the privilege of mine honours,

My oath, and my profession: I protest,

Maugre thy strength, youth, place, and
eminence,

Despite thy victor sword and fire-new fortune,

Thy valour and thy heart, thou art a traitor;

False to thy gods, thy brother, and thy father;

Conspirant 'gainst this high-illustrious prince;

And, from the extremest upward of thy head

To the descent and dust below thy foot,

A most toad-spotted traitor. Say thou 'No,'

This sword, this arm, and my best spirits, are

bent

To prove upon thy heart, whereto I speak,

Thou liest.

EDMUND: In wisdom I should ask thy name;

But, since thy outside looks so fair and warlike,

And that thy tongue some say of breeding

breathes,

What safe and nicely I might well delay

By rule of knighthood, I disdain and spurn:

Back do I toss these treasons to thy head;

With the hell-hated lie o'erwhelm thy heart;

Which, for they yet glance by and scarcely

bruise,

This sword of mine shall give them instant way,

Where they shall rest for ever. Trumpets, speak!

[*Alarums. They fight. EDMUND falls*]

ALBANY: Save him, save him!

GONERIL: This is practice, Gloucester:

By the law of arms thou wast not bound to

answer

An unknown opposite; thou art not vanquish'd,

But cozen'd and beguiled.

ALBANY: Shut your mouth, dame,

Or with this paper shall I stop it: Hold, sir:

Thou worse than any name, read thine own evil:

No tearing, lady: I perceive you know it.

[*Gives the letter to EDMUND*]

GONERIL: Say, if I do, the laws are mine, not

thine:

Who can arraign me for't.

ALBANY: Most monstrous! oh!

Know'st thou this paper?

GONERIL: Ask me not what I know.

[*Exit*]

ALBANY: Go after her: she's desperate; govern

her.

EDMUND: What you have charged me with, that

have I done;

And more, much more; the time will bring it out:

'Tis past, and so am I. But what art thou

That hast this fortune on me? If thou'rt noble,

I do forgive thee.

EDGAR: Let's exchange charity.

I am no less in blood than thou art, Edmund;

If more, the more thou hast wrong'd me.

My name is Edgar, and thy father's son.

The gods are just, and of our pleasant vices
Make instruments to plague us:
The dark and vicious place where thee he got
Cost him his eyes.

EDMUND: Thou hast spoken right, 'tis true;
The wheel is come full circle: I am here.

ALBANY: Methought thy very gait did prophesy
A royal nobleness: I must embrace thee:
Let sorrow split my heart, if ever I
Did hate thee or thy father!

EDGAR: Worthy prince, I know't.

ALBANY: Where have you hid yourself?
How have you known the miseries of your
father?

EDGAR: By nursing them, my lord. List a brief
tale;
And when 'tis told, O, that my heart would burst!
The bloody proclamation to escape,
That follow'd me so near,—O, our lives'
sweetness!
That we the pain of death would hourly die
Rather than die at once!—taught me to shift
Into a madman's rags; to assume a semblance
That very dogs disdain'd: and in this habit

Met I my father with his bleeding rings,

Their precious stones new lost: became his

guide,

Led him, begg'd for him, saved him from despair;

Never,–O fault!–reveal'd myself unto him,

Until some half-hour past, when I was arm'd:

Not sure, though hoping, of this good success,

I ask'd his blessing, and from first to last

Told him my pilgrimage: but his flaw'd heart,

Alack, too weak the conflict to support!

'Twixt two extremes of passion, joy and grief,

Burst smilingly.

EDMUND: This speech of yours hath moved me,

And shall perchance do good: but speak you on;

You look as you had something more to say.

ALBANY: If there be more, more woeful, hold it

in;

For I am almost ready to dissolve,

Hearing of this.

EDGAR: This would have seem'd a period

To such as love not sorrow; but another,

To amplify too much, would make much more,

And top extremity.

Whilst I was big in clamour came there in a man,

Who, having seen me in my worst estate,

Shunn'd my abhorr'd society; but then, finding

Who 'twas that so endured, with his strong arms

He fastened on my neck, and bellow'd out

As he'ld burst heaven; threw him on my father;

Told the most piteous tale of Lear and him

That ever ear received: which in recounting

His grief grew puissant and the strings of life

Began to crack: twice then the trumpets sounded,

And there I left him tranced.

ALBANY: But who was this?

EDGAR: Kent, sir, the banish'd Kent; who in disguise

Follow'd his enemy king, and did him service

Improper for a slave.

[*Enter a Gentleman, with a bloody knife*]

Gentleman: Help, help, O, help!

EDGAR: What kind of help?

ALBANY: Speak, man.

EDGAR: What means that bloody knife?

Gentleman: 'Tis hot, it smokes;

It came even from the heart of–O, she's dead!

ALBANY: Who dead? speak, man.

Gentleman: Your lady, sir, your lady: and her sister

By her is poisoned; she hath confess'd it.

EDMUND: I was contracted to them both: all three

Now marry in an instant.

EDGAR: Here comes Kent.

ALBANY: Produce their bodies, be they alive or dead:

This judgment of the heavens, that makes us tremble,

Touches us not with pity.

[*Exit Gentleman*]

[*Enter KENT*]

O, is this he?

The time will not allow the compliment

Which very manners urges.

KENT: I am come

To bid my king and master aye good night:

Is he not here?

ALBANY: Great thing of us forgot!

Speak, Edmund, where's the king? and where's Cordelia?

See'st thou this object, Kent?

[*The bodies of GONERIL and REGAN are brought in*]

KENT: Alack, why thus?

EDMUND: Yet Edmund was beloved:

The one the other poison'd for my sake,

And after slew herself.

ALBANY: Even so. Cover their faces.

EDMUND: I pant for life: some good I mean to do,

Despite of mine own nature. Quickly send,

Be brief in it, to the castle; for my writ

Is on the life of Lear and on Cordelia:

Nay, send in time.

ALBANY: Run, run, O, run!

EDGAR: To who, my lord? Who hath the office? send

Thy token of reprieve.

EDMUND: Well thought on: take my sword,

Give it the captain.

ALBANY: Haste thee, for thy life.

[*Exit EDGAR*]

EDMUND: He hath commission from thy wife and me

To hang Cordelia in the prison, and

To lay the blame upon her own despair,

That she fordid herself.

ALBANY: The gods defend her! Bear him hence
awhile.

[*EDMUND is borne off*]

[*Re-enter LEAR, with CORDELIA dead in his
arms; EDGAR, Officer, and Others*]

LEAR: Howl, howl, howl, howl! O, you are men
of stones:

Had I your tongues and eyes, I'ld use them so

That heaven's vault should crack. She's gone for
ever!

I know when one is dead, and when one lives;

She's dead as earth. Lend me a looking-glass;

If that her breath will mist or stain the stone,

Why, then she lives.

KENT: Is this the promised end

EDGAR: Or image of that horror?

ALBANY: Fall, and cease!

LEAR: This feather stirs; she lives! if it be so,

It is a chance which does redeem all sorrows

That ever I have felt.

KENT: [Kneeling] O my good master!

LEAR: Prithee, away.

EDGAR: 'Tis noble Kent, your friend.

LEAR: A plague upon you, murderers, traitors all!

I might have saved her; now she's gone for ever!

Cordelia, Cordelia! stay a little. Ha!

What is't thou say'st? Her voice was ever soft,

Gentle, and low, an excellent thing in woman.

I kill'd the slave that was a-hanging thee.

Officer: 'Tis true, my lords, he did.

LEAR: Did I not, fellow?

I have seen the day, with my good biting falchion

I would have made them skip: I am old now,

And these same crosses spoil me. Who are you?

Mine eyes are not o' the best: I'll tell you straight.

KENT: If fortune brag of two she loved and hated,

One of them we behold.

LEAR: This is a dull sight. Are you not Kent?

KENT: The same,

Your servant Kent: Where is your servant Caius?

LEAR: He's a good fellow, I can tell you that;

He'll strike, and quickly too: he's dead and rotten.

KENT: No, my good lord; I am the very man,—

LEAR: I'll see that straight.

KENT: That, from your first of difference and decay,

Have follow'd your sad steps.

LEAR: You are welcome hither.

KENT: Nor no man else: all's cheerless, dark, and deadly.

Your eldest daughters have fordone them selves,

And desperately are dead.

LEAR: Ay, so I think.

ALBANY: He knows not what he says: and vain it is

That we present us to him.

EDGAR: Very bootless.

[*Enter an Officer*]

Officer: Edmund is dead, my lord.

ALBANY: That's but a trifle here.

You lords and noble friends, know our intent.

What comfort to this great decay may come

Shall be applied: for us we will resign,

During the life of this old majesty,

To him our absolute power:

To EDGAR and KENT]

you, to your rights:

With boot, and such addition as your honours

Have more than merited. All friends shall taste
The wages of their virtue, and all foes
The cup of their deservings. O, see, see!

LEAR: And my poor fool is hang'd! No, no, no life!
Why should a dog, a horse, a rat, have life,
And thou no breath at all? Thou'lt come no more,
Never, never, never, never, never!
Pray you, undo this button: thank you, sir.
Do you see this? Look on her, look, her lips,
Look there, look there!
[*Dies*]

EDGAR: He faints! My lord, my lord!

KENT: Break, heart; I prithee, break!

EDGAR: Look up, my lord.

KENT: Vex not his ghost: O, let him pass! he hates him much
That would upon the rack of this tough world
Stretch him out longer.

EDGAR: He is gone, indeed.

KENT: The wonder is, he hath endured so long:
He but usurp'd his life.

ALBANY: Bear them from hence. Our present business

Is general woe.

[*To KENT and EDGAR*]

Friends of my soul, you twain

Rule in this realm, and the gored state sustain.

KENT: I have a journey, sir, shortly to go;

My master calls me, I must not say no.

ALBANY: The weight of this sad time we must obey;

Speak what we feel, not what we ought to say.

The oldest hath borne most: we that are young

Shall never see so much, nor live so long.

[*Exeunt, with a dead march*]

My Notes

Glossary of Literary Terms

Alliteration: The occurrence of identical sounds, most often at the beginning of words e.g. "From forth the fatal loins of these two foes"

Allusion: An indirect reference to something

Anaphora: Repetition of the same word or phrase at the beginning of consecutive lines

Antagonist: The **protagonist**'s main adversary.

Antithesis: A person or thing that is the opposite of something else

Aside: A character's remark that is only meant to be heard by the audience but unheard by other characters in the play

Assonance: The resemblance of sounds between vowels of words in close proximity to one another

Blank verse: **Poetry** written with a regular **metre** but unrhymed, almost always in **iambic pentameter**

Climax: The dramatic end to the main **plot**. This is usually followed by **falling action**

Couplet: Two successive rhyming lines

Dramatic monologue: A poem in the form of a speech of an individual character

Euphemism: A gentle way of expressing something unpleasant

Falling Action: The section of a story following the **climax** but before the very end of the story

Foil: A character providing a contrast with another

Foot: A combination of stressed and unstressed syllables

Heroic couplet: a pair of rhyming **iambic pentameters**

Hyperbole: Exaggerated statements not meant to be taken literally

Iambic pentameter: A line of verse with five metrical feet, each consisting of one unstressed syllable followed by one stressed syllable

Imagery: A visually descriptive use of language

Internal rhyme: A rhyme involving a word in the middle of a line

Metaphor: A figure of speech that applies words to describe something in a non-literal way (e.g. *coal black eyes*). Metaphors do not use the words "like" or "as". If these words are used it is a **simile** (e.g. *eyes as black as coal*, or *eyes like black coal*).

Metre: The basic rhythmic structure of a verse or lines in a verse

Motif: An image or idea that runs through a play or novel

Onomatopoeia: A word that resembles the sound it is describing e.g. cuckoo, woof, burp, etc

Oxymoron: A figure of speech containing contradictory words, e.g. deafening silence

Paradox: A statement that contradicts itself e.g "This sentence is not true"

Personification: Attributing human characteris-tics to inanimate things

Plot: The events that make up the main part of a story

Poetry: Rhymed or rhythmic text

Pronoun: Referring to a person or thing, e.g. I, you, she, this, that

Prose: Written or spoken language without rhyme or rhythm

Protagonist: The lead character

Quatrain: A **stanza** of four lines

Refrain: A word or series of words repeated at intervals within a poem

Shakespearean sonnet: A fourteen-line poem written in **iambic pentameter**, composed of three **quatrains** of four lines each and a **couplet** rhyming: abab cdcd efef gg.

Simile: A figure of speech containing "as" or "like" to describe something in a non-literal way (e.g. eyes like black coal). If the words "like" or "as" are not used then it is a **metaphor** (e.g. coal black eyes).

Soliloquy: A speech spoken by a character when alone, revealing their innermost thoughts

Sonnet: A fourteen-line poem. See also **Shakespearean sonnet**

Stanza: A group of poetic lines resembling paragraphs in **prose**

Sub-plot: A plot separate to the main **plot**

Syntax: The arrangement of words and phrases within a sentence

Tragic Hero: Generally the **protagonist** whose flaws or mistakes lead to their downfall

King Lear Glossary

Arbitrement – The final decision made by an arbitrator
Avouched – Affirmed
Ballow – A cudgel or thick stick
Bemadding – Maddening
Benison – A blessing
Besort – Appropriate
Cadent – Falling
Carbonado – Cut
Century – A military unit
Conceit – Excessive pride
Cowish – Cowardly
Coxcomb – A cap, often worn by jester
Cullionly – Contemptible (cullion means testicle)
Dog-hearted – Pitiless
Faith'd – Believed
Felicitate – Made happy
Festinate – Hasten
Finical – Fussy
Fitchew – A polecat (a weasel which had a reputation for being both smelly and lecherous)
Fordone – Destroyed
Forfended – Forbidden
Gauntlet – Medieval glove
Goatish – Lecherous
Jakes – Outdoor toilet
Justicer – Judge
Kibe – Swelling, especially on the heel
Maugre – In spite of
Meiny – Household attendants
Minikin – Small

Moiety – A half share
Opposeless – Irresistible
Placket – Pocket
Propinquity – Closely related
Questrist – Seeker
Recreant – Unfaithful or cowardly
Simple – A herb used on its own for medical treatment
Smilet – Small smile
Snuffs – Disputes
Squiny – Squint
Trundle-tail – Curly-tailed dog
Vaunt-couriers – A herald, or someone sent in advance
Yoke-fellow – Close companion

For more on our large print, dyslexia-friendly, and annotation-friendly books, as well as our bulk discounts for schools visit:

firestonebooks.com

Printed in Great Britain
by Amazon

48195725R00121